Design

ridge

Home Product Design

arco
editorial

AUTHOR
Francisco Asensio Cerver

PUBLISHING DIRECTOR
Paco Asensio

PROJECT CO-ORDINATOR
Anna Puyuelo (Architect)

TRANSLATION
David Buss

DESIGN & LAYOUT
Mireia Casanovas Soley

PHOTOGRAPHERS
Globus (*Pepe Cortés*); Javier Sardá (*F.J.Barba Corsini*); Cocha Prada,
Enrique Carrazoni, Miro Zagnoli, Remigio M. Vilaplana (*Sandra
Figuerola y Marisa Gallén*); Aldo Ballo (*Angelo Mangiarotti*);
William Taylor, Richard Speedy, Marek Bulaj (*Michael Graves*);
Emilio Tremola (*Pierangelo Caramia*); Ole Woldbye, Erik Hagens
(*Ursula Munch-Petersen*); Luciano Soave, Aldo Ballo (*Achille
Castiglioni*); Ole Akhøj (*Ole Jensen*); Luciano Soave, Santi Caleca,
Gionata Xerra, Aldo Ballo, Louisiana (*Vico Magistretti*); Tom Vack
(*Konstantin Grcic, Axel Kufus*); Tom Vack, Hans Hansen (*Franz
Josef Schultz*)

Copyright © 1997 Arco Editorial SA
ISBN: 2-88046-297-5

Published and distributed by RotoVision SA
Sheridan House
112-116A Western Road
Hove, East Sussex BN3 1DD
England
Tel. 1273 72 72 68
Fax. 1273 72 72 69

Production and color separation in Singapore by
ProVision Pte. Ltd.
Tel. (65) 334-7720
Fax (65) 334-7721

10 F.J. Barba Corsini 16 Siegfried Bensinger 20 Marcus Botsch 24 Pierangelo Caramia 30 Achille Castiglioni 38 Pepe Cortés 42 Rodolfo Dordoni 48 Sandra Figuerola y Marisa Gallén 54 Michael Graves 60 Konstantin Grcic 64 Ole Jensen 68 Axel Kufus 72 Herbert Ludwikowski 80 Vico Magistretti 84 Peter Maly 88 Angelo Mangiarotti 94 Javier Mariscal 100 Nani Marquina 106 Ursula Munch-Petersen 110 André Ricard 118 Núria Robert 128 Franz Josef Schulte 132 Philippe Starck 140 Òscar Tusquets 148 Norbert Wangen

Home Product Design

Industrial design, like other artistic disciplines, has undergone variations during the course of time and has been the expression of different values at different times.

During the nineteenth century, design reflected the appreciation of the painstaking work of the craftsman and the value of manual skills. Later, with the industrial revolution, design became the expression of the new methods of production of a society trying to come to terms with a new way of doing things based on mass production and the profit motive. There have even been times during or after wars, when industrial design has been used as one more sign of national prestige or as a representative image of a certain ideology.

Today, like other artistic forms, design is not at the service of any particular ideology, but rather has become the expression of the individuality of the artist and a reflection of the new materials and methods of production that have become available. Design is now treated as an added value and applied according to market demand. This means that the relationship between creator and producer is ever more crucial. The objects we see in the shops have to pass through the unforgiving filter of the producing firms and the final result depends on their talent.

The approach to a design piece is personal, both on the part of the creator and the user. Unlike a cooking recipe which guarantees good results, there are no dogmas or parameters to guide us as to what is good and what is bad. What we can do is try to recognise the emotive aspect of the object and the capacity it has for dialogue with the materials, its use and its user.

A dialogue in which all the parties implicated - designer, object and user - have the same importance and must have an active approach, as in spite of its apparent simplicity, it is fragile and easily frustrated during any part of the process if there is no interest.

Perhaps these ideas may serve as an orientation with respect to the diversity of approaches to design which exist today, and of which this book attempts to present a sample.

Home Product Design

F.J. Barba Corsini

The collection of furniture shown here was designed and produced in response to a commission received by the architect F.J.Barba Corsini at the beginning of the 50's to remodel the attic floor of the building known as La Pedrera (Arch. A. Gaudí). The property company which owned La Pedrera in 1955, wished to profit from the empty spaces of the highest floor of the building, which from the beginning had been used for storage and laundry. Thus it was decided to transform the space into small apartments for rent, each one having access to a small private terrace. The idea seemed to have every chance of success, as at the time this type of housing, the urban "apartment" was thought to be fashionable.

The project consisted of thirteen apartments (although numbered 1 to 14 for reasons of superstition), located on the one floor of this Barcelona landmark, with fabulous views of the city. The renovation was not limited solely to the design of the architectural spaces, but also included the creation of a whole series of exclusive pieces of furniture. The plan in its entirety defined not just the distribution and spacial relation between the pieces, but also the image and the form of use imposed by this special furniture.

Barba Corsini's design for the project used an original constructive solution based on parabolic partition arches which allowed the rising height of the space to be fully utilized by the incorporation of platforms. The architect's identification with the building was especially intense and he did not decide upon the use of any material, shape or distribution without testing his ideas *in situ*. Models were reproduced in brick; samples of materials were tested in the spaces they would occupy, and even full-scale models were made of the stairs in wire and the chairs in cardboard.

Any renovation of a building with the personality and almost symbolic meaning of "La Pedrera" is not an easy task. However, in this case, the plan, both architecturally and in the design of the furnishings, showed a clear autonomy with respect to the work of Gaudí, with no trace of imitation. An article published in the newspaper "Diario de Barcelona" on the 17th July 1955, clearly expresses this idea:

"Any alterations in a house designed by Gaudí are always a delicate matter. This original and bold architect was an innovator of genius, and has

Lamp formed by a cylinder of perforated sheet iron with a Y-shaped strut which reinforces the cylinder and supports the electrical components. The rounded feet are also soldered to the strut.

Wall-lamp in the form of a flattened and inverted cone laterally fixed to a cylindrical band which attaches to the wall. The electrical components are inside the lamp.

Chair constructed of an oval seat-back rest in one piece, supported by two inverted U-shape tubes, which incline sharply outwards to the floor.

a legion of followers who are extremely conservative and cry to the heavens as soon as they get a whiff of any idea to move even one brick of the houses built by their idol.

"La Pedrera" has avoided the problem by leaving the exterior untouched. Within the building, two worlds live together. The twisted and tormented world of Gaudí and the clear, straight, clean world of functionalism. The spirit of Gaudí blends harmoniously with that of Barba Corsini, the architect who authored the transformation. The undulating floor, the partition arches of the house, his decorative extravagances and his structural oddities seem to be conceived precisely for this almost cinematographic atmosphere".

Barba Corsini understood this project in terms of "Interior Architecture" which means working freely in the three dimensions of the space, as opposed to the idea of "interior design" which lends itself to the decoration of two flat dimensions.

It was within the context of this plan that the furniture shown on these pages was conceived.

S-shaped bench whose seat is formed by a series of circular shaped pieces of wood in different tones, supported by an horizontal L-shaped structure of iron, which follows the shape of the bench, and is attached to the vertical tubular feet.

The character of the spaces for which the furniture was to be used did not hinder Barba Corsini in designing pieces with their own presence. The pieces were produced by Galeria H2O in 1995, forty years after they were originally designed in . 1955, but have not lost any of their immediacy.

The furniture is capable of generating a determined atmosphere around it, independent of

where it is placed, as rather than imposing their
materiality, they have a somewhat indefinable
appeal. They speak of the quality of the light, of
smooth oundulating lines that are sensitive to the
user, of the delicacy with which the contact points
between the object and the supporting structure
are constructed, of a manner of seeking support
from the floor by vertices that almost flee from
the horizontal plane. ●

Table with a glass surface composed
of contoured arched pieces,
supported by the upper vertices of
the tubular V-shaped understructure.

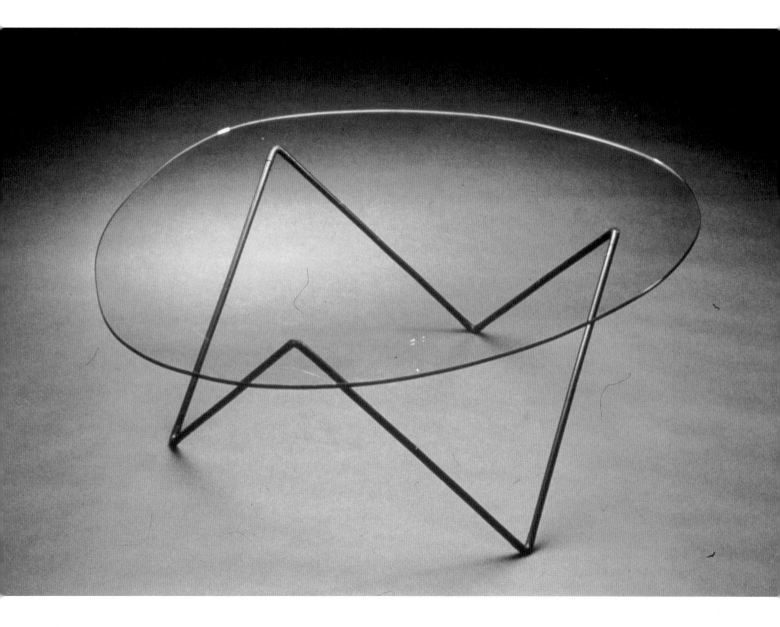

"Tatami"
A bedroom concept designed and
developed during the years
1988-1991. Production:
Interlübke.

Siegfried Bensinger

A "tatami" is a type of rush matting
traditionally used as a floor covering in Japanese
houses. As shoes are always left in the entrance
hall and not worn in the house, the tatami is
always kept free of the dirt from outside, and is
thus usable for all types of household activity. A
thin mattress is placed over it for sleeping, and
people sit on it to eat from low tables, to chat or
to watch television.

It is not at all strange that it is this Japanese
word "tatami" with its insinuations of another
culture, and other forms of daily life that has been
chosen as the name for the type of bedroom
created by Bensinger.

"Tatami" is a reflection of more than just the
Japanese word. "Tatami" speaks of the horizontal
nature of Japanese domestic architecture, where a
low observation point relaxes the mind, and also
of the mobility which is the essence of a room in
which nothing is permanently fixed and
everything may be modified: the movable bed is
homologous to the sliding rice-paper partition
panels. "Tatami" reminds us that it is possible to
sleep in a different way from that which we are

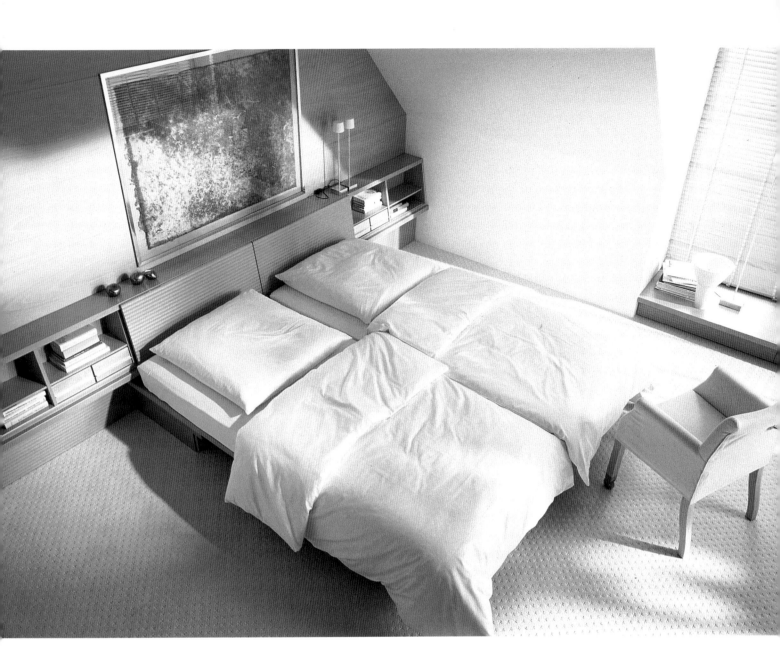

accustomed to, and that a double bed does not always have to be the same thing, and offers the possibility of deciding at any time the layout of the bedroom and the relation between its occupants.

Simplicity of line, in which no element is purely an accessory, clarity of concept and the natural materials are inescapably Japanese characteristics translated into a design which makes no concession to clichéd ideas of what is Japanese, but which pursues and achieves its aim by an analysis of the essence of concepts alien to Western culture, and which, included here, lead to a new approach to the idea of sleeping.•

"Tatami" gives movement to the bedroom: a double bed easily converts into two single beds, sliding along rails hidden under the bolster. The beds can be of different widths: 90, 100, & 120cm.

The basic element of this design is the large, low bases, which hide the rails for the sliding beds and can incorporate drawers.

The system also allows the fixation of shelves of variable heights and dimensions which adapt to the needs of the user, making flexibility the essence of this design.

18

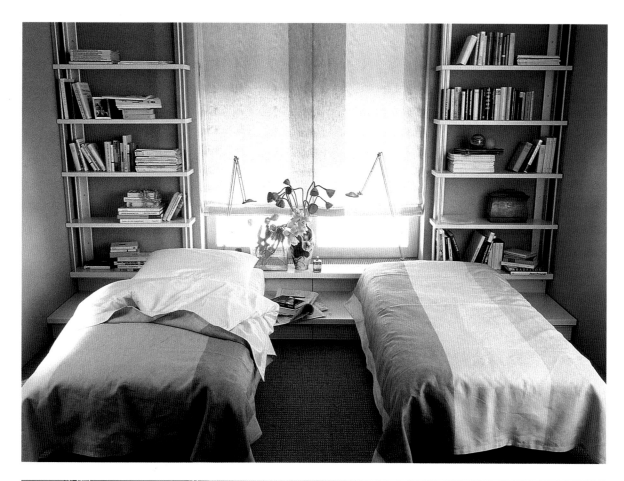

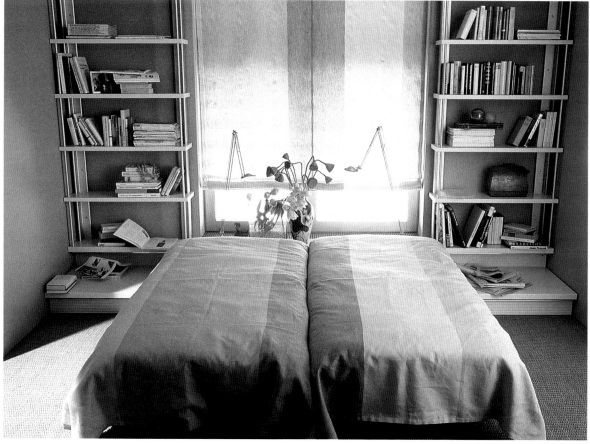

Marcus Botsch

Marcus Botsch studied precision mechanics before graduating in industrial design from the University of Essen. This academic training, unusual for a designer, has given him a different vision of his profession, focusing on materials and methods of anchoring them, and manufacturing systems.

Any attempt to analyse the forms proposed by this German designer using his academic background may seem gratuitous, but what is undeniable is the knowledge of materials and the methods of joining them that he demonstrates. Once again we find ourselves confronted with objects that are voluntarily minimal and neutral with a mechanical aesthetic whose coldness and

impersonality is broken by subtle touches. This is emphasized by the treatment that the metal sheets receive. These are folded and manipulated as if they were made of paper, in a style reminiscent of Japanese origami. In origami, perfectly squared pieces of paper are folded in a predetermined way which transforms the bi-dimensional sheets into small sculptures as if by magic.

Botsch does the same with the metallic surfaces of his "Hängecontainer", folding and manipulating them in such a way that it is possible to forget the mechanical process needed to achieve these results, and then fixing them to each other and to the wall in the simplest possible way. Once in place, this cupboard-container for

"Hängecontainer" (1989). Production: Nils Holger Moormann.
Front view of this hanging cupboard which was awarded a prize in 1990 by the Design Zentrum of Nordrhein Westfalen.

The piece expands from above by means of the easily assembled square containers suspended one above another. The height of the unit is variable depending on the number of modules used.

"Hängecontainer" (1989). Production: Nils Holger Moormann.
Detail of the wall-fixture.
The modules are made from steel sheeting finished in various colours.

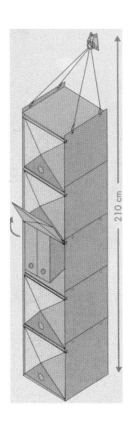

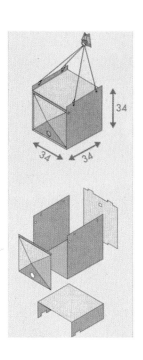

various objects almost floats, fleeing from gravity and underlining the slightness of the folded metal sheets.

One example is the P.A.P. wastebasket. This is composed of three identical sheets and a base, all of steel, and uses the minimum amount of material and the maximum amount of simplicity in the joins. But there is a small detail which makes the P.A.P. something more than just a well-resolved commercial object: the three vertical slots in the sides. This simple addition transforms the P.A.P. into a Japanese style "origami", that is, steel sheets simply folded and trimmed as if they were paper. In addition the slots allow us to see how full the wastebasket is. •

Pierangelo Caramia

Caramia, an Italian architect living in Paris, a collaborator of Philippe Starck for a period, is a cosmopolitan and wide-ranging designer. His works have been produced in countries as different as Italy, France and Japan by companies with very different lines: Cassina, Alessi, Xo, Doublet, Constantino, etc.

The objects designed by Pierangelo Caramia for Constantino express a close relationship between the industrial and the artisanal, and this implies a specific philosophy and method of production so that his objects reach the market without losing the ideas and intentions with which they were generated. His designs are very aware of the methods of production and industrial logic in assuring the rationality of the process, and at the same time do not lose sight of the experimentation which is necessary to ensure that the craftsman can use his manual skills with materials to the best advantage.

Caramia, an architect, suggests that his creations are a testament to our contemporary culture, and in his own words, try to improve, even if modestly, the quality of life: his table objects invite care in the presentation of the table and the table made of the same ceramic material

"Trevi" (1991)
Produced by Cassina.
A low, eliptic table made of
pearl-grey lacquered wood
which can be adjusted in
height thanks to pedal-
controlled gas pressure.

"Tabula" table and "Aura" chair. (1996)
The table has a beechwood structure
and a ceramic surface.
The chair is also of beech and is finished
in pear-wood. The removable cushion is
of leather.
Produced for Constantino, for whose
collection "Industria & artigiani"
Caramia was at the time artistic
director.

"Only wood" table. (1992)
Produced by Xo. Artistic director of the
collection: Philippe Stark.

"Penguin" (1993)
Stainless steel jar with handle and base
in blue polyamide. Height: 23cm., 120cl.
for Alessi.

"Penguin Tea" (1993)
Stainless steel teapot with handle and
base in green polyamide. Height: 23cm.
120cl., for Alessi.

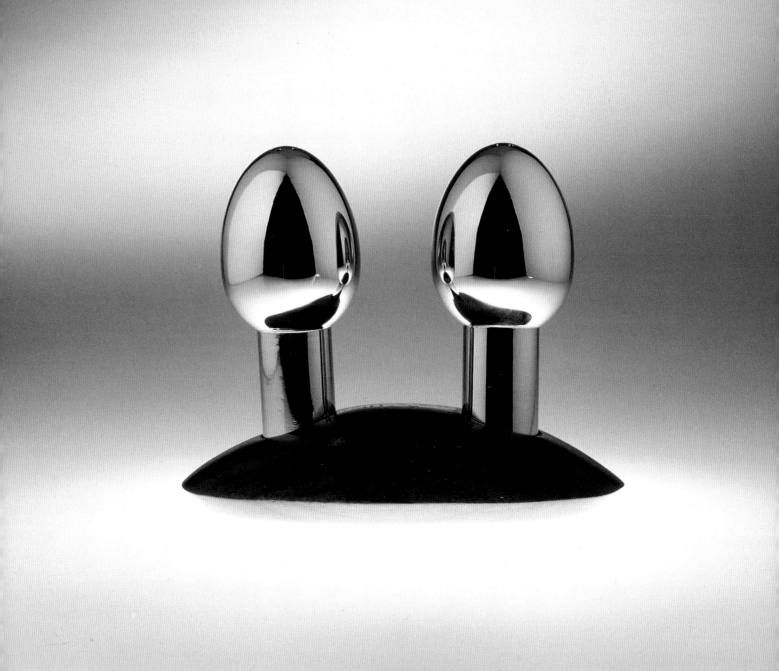

"Rio" (1992)
Salt and pepper pots of stainless steel, with
wooden cruet, produced by Alessi.
Dimensions: 12.5 x 8cm. Height: 9.5cm.

as the plates invites us to eat better.

What we are dealing with here are clear, and simple designs which take into account the basic components of the design process, the impact they will make when used, experimentation with materials and techniques, and finally, the inclusion of the methods of production.

In the objects designed for Xo, the materials and finishes are completely different. There is an explosion of colours associated with the furniture

"Black Josephine" (1995)
Biscuit-box in crystal with stainless steel lid
and handle of SAN, produced for Alessi.
Dimensions: 21x 12cm. Height: 22cm.

of the second half of the century, an optimistic and confident aesthetic. The Pigalle chair from 1995 is available in various colours such as violet, apple green and earth tones. The objects for Alessi – salt and pepper pots, teapots and milk jars – are full of irony and anecdote. The teapot or milk jar with their egg- shaped form, leaning slightly on tiny feet, bring to mind a penguin with its peculiar clumsy gait. •

Achille Castiglioni

Achille Castiglioni's experience in industrial design goes back to his first efforts in the field in 1940, together with his brothers Livio and Pier Giacomo. In 1969 he began his academic career at the Polytechnic University of Turin, teaching a course in "Artistic design for Industry", an activity which he continues today.

This direct relationship with the University throughout his career has defined an approach to industrial design based on constant study and research. According to Castiglione, the quality of a product can be measured by its innovative capacity, understood not as a banal search for formal or commercial novelty at all costs, but as the discovery of some kind of real inventiveness.

The design must deviate from the norm and go further than the expectations of the client or the market. The important thing is never to base ideas on data generated by market surveys as these only reflect stereotypes, images already assimilated by the public, which cannot serve as the foundation of any innovative project.

The problem is that while in other times the basic research which marked the steps to be followed in the development of a product was the

*"Brera" hanging lamp. (1992)
A hanging lamp composed of a
rose-shaped support, a steel
suspension cable, two electric cables
with a socket and an ovoid shade
made of acid-etched blown glass.*

*"Brera" wall lamp. (1992)
The special way the pieces are
joined allows the position of the
characteristic glass shade to be
inverted, which means that the
same shade can be used for
different types of lamps: wall,
table, free-standing, hanging
or embedded.*

responsibility of the designer, today it is in the hands of the manufacturers. These firms have at their disposition ever more complex economic and organizational resources and their criteria are based on increasing demand at any price, with consumption as the only reference. In Castiglioni's own words, "the designer who conforms to this behaviour is not working to improve the quality of life, but only for financial gain, and is therefore making no effort to positively modify the environment".

The designer should follow a line which encourages criticism and constructive dialogue with the client, who thus becomes implicated in the artistic doubts and concerns which are the motor of the design process.

For this Italian architect, a good design should always deny what already exists, raising the threshold of expectation both of the client and the market.

In the light of these ideas, the designer is seen as a permanent investigator, who, far from adhering to a comfortable theoretical position,

"Brera" table lamp. (1992)
The continuity of light intensity is guaranteed by the separation of the shade into two parts, allowing the bulb and the socket to cool rapidly.

"Scrittarello"
Small table or writing desk with side panels of plywood finished in beech or white laminate, produced for è De Padova.

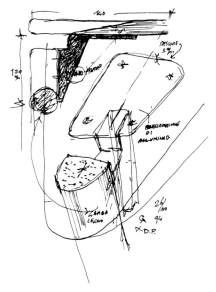

Detail of the join between the legs and
the table-top of Tavolo'95. The space
which results from this join lightens the
table and the table-top appears to float
above the legs.

Tavolo'95
Table with wooden chipboard legs and
aluminium supports. The table-top comes
in various forms (circular, square or
rectangular) and various finishes (white
laminated wood, marble or maple).
Production: è De Padova.

"Mate"
Tray with folding support in natural
beechwood or dyed in a cherry colour.
Support made from strips of blue
cotton. Production: è De Padova.

ensures that his methodology evolves in time
with the economic and productive circumstances
of the reality in which he lives.

Castiglioni's teaching duties, which have
constituted a direct relationship with the
University, throughout his career, are indicative of
the vitality of his position with respect to design,
based on constant study and research, enabling
him to maintain a critical position at all times.

Quoting Castiglioni, "Design is not a
discipline, but a stance born as the result of a
personal formation based on humanistic,

35

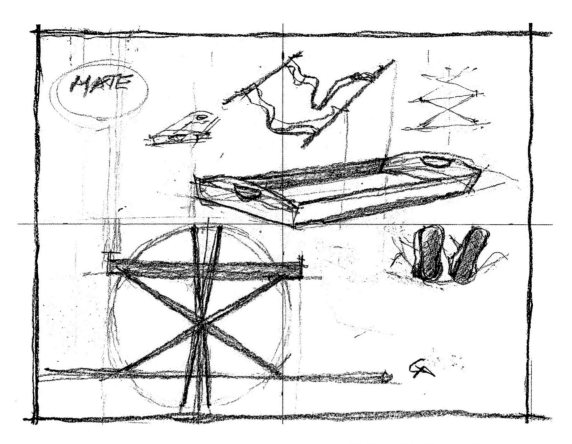

*Working model which studies the way
in which the auxiliary tray folds up.*

*"Mini Mate/Super Mate"
Tray with folding support in natural
beechwood or dyed in a cherry colour.
Production: è De Padova.*

"Fix"
Stoolseat with a steel structure painted with polyurethane powder. Its simplicity and different sizes make it very versatile. Production: é De Padova.

Detail of the cushions of the "Fix" seat in cotton cloth.

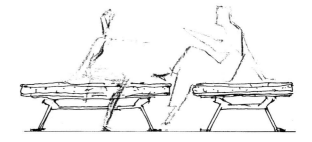

technological, economic and political criticism".

His recent designs form part of this ongoing scientific investigation related to the process of integral design, that is, the study of the interdisciplinary relationship between the various operative phases as an integration of the language between production and culture.

The result of this study is that his designs show great maturity in the use of materials and of the linking pieces between the parts which, with very little variation from the norm, succeed in changing the perception of the objects completely and multiplying their uses. •

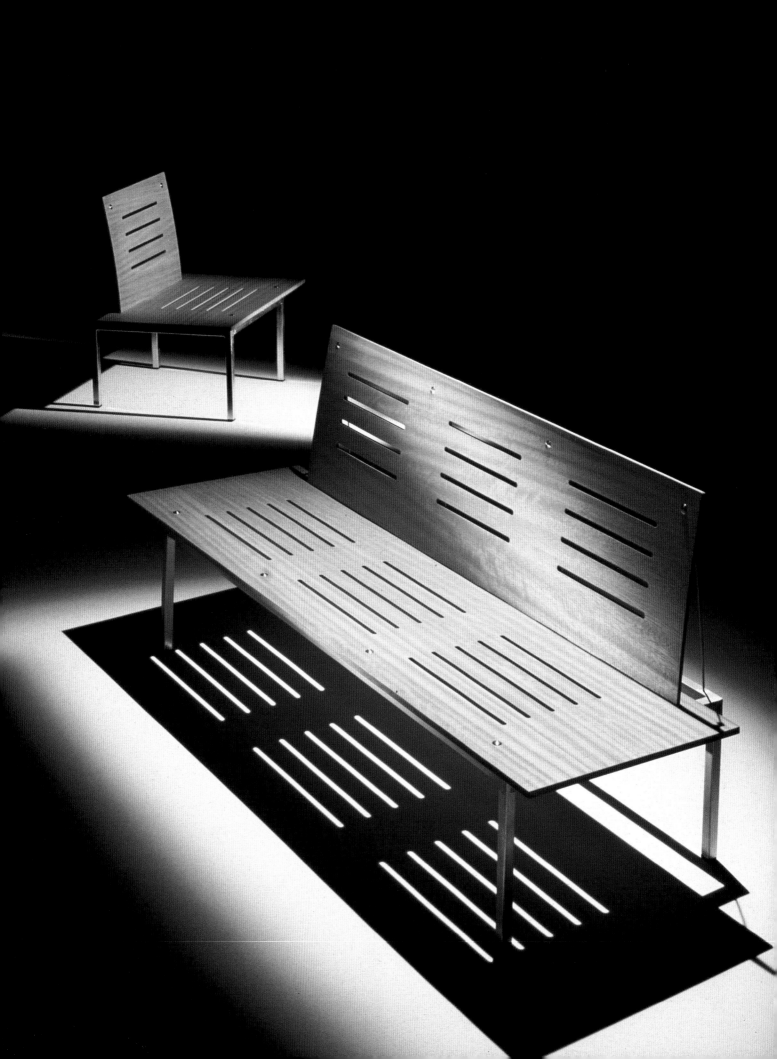

Pepe Cortés

The latest work of Pepe Cortés in both industrial and interior design has shown a marked change in his way of thinking.

After many years of collaboration with architects and designers such as Javier Mariscal, Alfredo Arribas, Eduard Samsó and Oscar Tusquets, Cortés has assumed the challenge of contemplating design from an exclusively individual point of view, distancing himself from the search for liberation through form that was the driving force of his earlier works. The disproportionate emphasis on form, readily accepted by the specialized magazines and the public, has, with the accumulation of experience, given way to a more realistic and conscious approach in his latest work, in which the study of proportion, permanence and subtlety are the keynotes.

Cortés has passed from the surprise and expressive exuberance of his earlier work to a style which is more contained and serene, and in which a desire that things last is patent.

According to Cortés, it is easy to fall into the trap of vulgarity when objects are designed solely on the basis of the entertainment aspect of the product, or its supposed modernity, both of which ensure a short life. To distance himself from vulgarity and fashion, and to give priority to the formal component of the work, Cortés tries, as far as is possible, to let his designs "sleep" for a few months, to see how they resist the passing of time. This strategy gives him a better perspective from which to consider the results, and if on a second examination he sees some aspect which is not essential, that is to say, purely fashionable, he can change the approach in order to purify the design

and obtain a product that is rational and tranquil.

However, Cortés has not forgotten the importance of ingenuity in the design process, and indeed this aspect is fundamental in all his work, but should be understood not only as formal creative ingenuity, but also as the use of new mechanisms, of unknown ideas, and of the application of techniques from other industries, which, decontextualized, generate new feelings and suggestions. The objective is, in short, to create new associations, both of ideas and techniques, which allow the creation of objects which satisfy productive requirements and communicate something to the user.

The works of Pep Cortés shown here, the "Gracia" bench and the "Jamaica" stool, are good examples of this attitude. In both, the study of productive techniques and materials serves as a base for reflection on the meaning of the word "sitting" which extends further than the materialistic nature of the realized concept.

We are not dealing with indifferent objects, insensitive to the user. Here the choice of materials and the surface of the seat offer the necessary path to follow in order to communicate with these objects.

The Gracia bench, designed for a terrace or garden, is based on a simple structure of metallic tubes which support a seat and back of grooved plywood which allows us to play with the feelings of what it means to sit in the exterior; the shadows which play over the floor, the cool feeling of a discontinuous surface. In addition, a series of other features (headrests, armrests, drinks holders) multiply the functions of the bench and personalise its use: sitting to have an aperitif, to read, to sunbathe or take a nap.

In the same way, the "Jamaica" stool plays with subtle shapes and materials, distancing itself from the rigidity of this type of seat. The rounded lines and the intrinsic qualities of the material seek the complicity of the user by giving comfort

"Jamaica" Stool. (1991)
Originally created as a one-off piece for a discoteque, it was later refined until arriving at the definitive form commercialized by Amat-3.

The seat is what makes the Jamaica a different type of stool. The rotating seat with its undulating shapes, designed to adapt to the human form with the maximum of comfort, contrasts with the hardness of the materials used.

The support of the stool consists of five sections of tubing which radiate out to the floor, and are joined by a metal band which acts as a footrest and ensures stability.

The feet and the seat are joined by a piece composed of a fixed disk which is screwed to the seat and a spindle which allows the seat to rotate.

as, more than any other objective of formal reference, the search for ergonometric correctness was the criteria that prevailed.●

The purposely simple and austered shapes of the "Jamaica" stool, together with the option of choosing aluminium or wood for the seat, make it a piece adaptable to any environment.

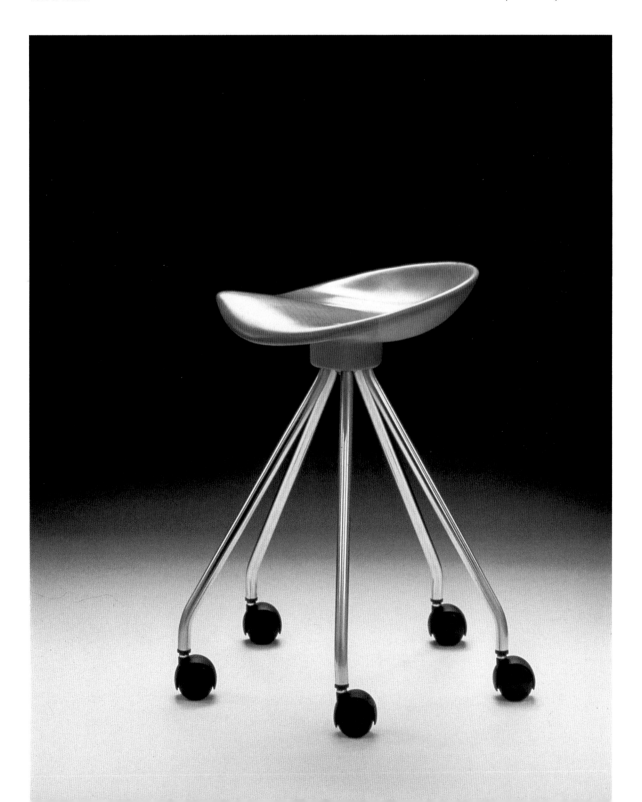

Rodolfo Dordoni

Many industrial designers were formally trained as architects. One example is Rodolfo Dordoni, an Italian architect born in Milan, who studied in the Polytechnic University of his native city.

The gestation and production of objects such as lamps and sofas is completely different from that of a building, and they are obviously used in different ways, but the way in which the projects are similar in both spheres has a common base, with the architect having to work with a change of scale. The architect, by training, is able to think in certain ways that are also essential on a smaller scale: a relationship with the surroundings and with the user, a structure that supports the object, a way of using it and a way of creating space.

Dordoni began his career as an architect, and changed to industrial design with the idea of defining a strategy in the world of images which allows him to go further than the product itself, and establish a dialogue with the user. His collaboration with so many companies in this field is testimony to the success of this idea which

"Paco" (1996) Produced by Flos.
A table lamp with diffused light. The shade is
composed of many mosaic pieces of polycarbonate in
different colours (amber, white, blue and green). Each
lamp comes with two sets of pieces for joining the
mosaic, one of the same colour, the other of a
different colour, giving a variety of chromatic
possibilities. The switch is phosphorescent, to aid
locating the lamp in the dark.
Dimensions: shade diameter, 12cm, height, 42cm.

"Oci" (1996).
Produced by Flos.
Table lamp with diffused
light. The shade is of
Murano blown-glass.
Dimensions: 18.5cm
wide, 80cm high.

Dordoni has tried to express in all the pieces he has designed.

Dordoni aligns himself with the general feeling of Italian design, expressing his discomfort with the principal tendencies of the market defined by the new production strategies for domestic furniture. This discomfort is the result of the everwider gap between the manufacturers acting in the name of a supposedly manipulable public and creative professionals. The objectives of the two sides are not irreconcilable but the unilateral definition of market strategy by the manufacturers is slowly limiting the creative work of designers who do not have the power to say what should be done.

Dordoni's theoretical vision is clear enough. According to him, there has been in recent times a new cultural enthusiasm which is related more to a re-evaluation of artisans work than with the techniques and rules of the industrial product. In some of his designs this idea is reflected by a progressive elimination of the components of the product, in line with systems of mass-production in which production in series is more important than any other idea. A search for the formal communicative essence of the object, which responds both to the concerns of the designer and to the methods of production. This is the case with the "Waiting" series of sofas in which the creative intensity is focused on the idea of a serial support system which is unique for any of the solutions. The seats can be adopted to various forms and configurations independently of the legs, as these have been designed to give the maximum freedom without compromising the functionability of the product. In this series of sofas, Dordoni shows his ability to bring together all the personal elements of his work whilst keeping in mind the necessities of production.

In contrast, some of his lamps seem to express values that are in contradiction to his

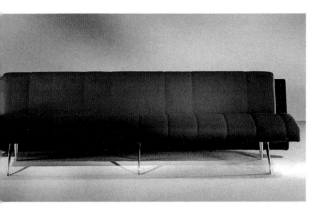

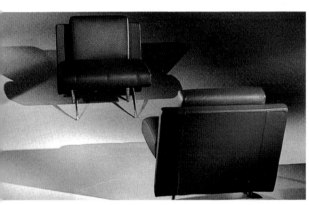

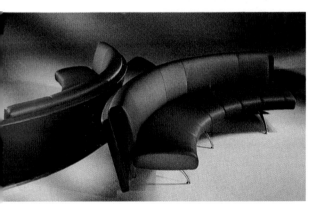

stated theoretical stance, as the expressive capacity of the materials, worked by age-old techniques is more important than considerations of massproduction. The reduction of the components of the piece as a base for an industrial product is not exactly the primordial objective of a piece such as the "Loca" lamp (models "Foglie" and "Fazzoletto") in which the hand-worked Murano glass is given priority.

This duality of stances which can be observed in Dordoni's work clearly expresses the difficulty of adhering to an initial theoretical outlook which may be modified by factors unconnected with the designer's wishes, and shows how creative criteria are sometimes determined by the type of commission received.●

"Waiting" (1989)

"Re" (1995).
A chair produced for
Muebles Moroso.

"Waiting" (1989)
A collection of chairs and sofas with the same formal idea and structure, but with variations in the dimensions and shapes.
Produced by Muebles Moroso.

"Loca" (1996). Model "Foglie". Produced by Flos.
Another Flos article is this ceiling-light with both diffused and direct light. The shade is of handworked Murano glass.
Leaf-shaped hanging lamps with a variety of colours and finishes.
Dimensions: Shade diameter 65cm. Height 40cm.

"Loca" (1996). Model "Fazzoletto". Produced by Flos.
A different model of ceiling-light, also with direct and diffused light, produced by Flos using handworked Murano glass in various colours and finishes.
Dimensions: Shade diameter 65cm. Height 35cm.

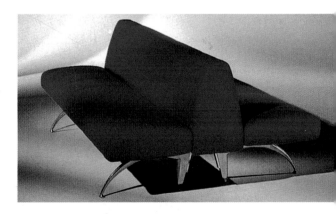

Sandra Figuerola & Marisa Gallén

"Our development is nourished by a wide range of artistic stimuli. We don't adhere excessively to any style or language. We believe that no style is absolute. In some cases, rationality is the most efficient and valuable answer, but in others passion and expressiveness is more indicated. It depends. Given the possibility of choosing one or another way of expression, isn't it more enriching to reserve the option of showing it in one way or another according to the circumstances, rather than tying oneself to the obligation of always using the same language, whatever the situation?

Our temperament points us towards a multidirectional focus rather than a pretence of specializing. This multiplicity allows the different fields to cross-breed in a system of systems in which everything is interrelated, permitting one to escape from the limited perspective of the specialized redoubt.

It could be thought that this multiplicity gyrates around only one subject: design in its different manifestations. Of these, there is one that especially interests us: the design of objects that belong to a household environment.

We think that we can contribute an ethic of the care of objects."

Sandra Figuerola & Marisa Gallén.

The studies carried out by both Sandra Figuerola and Marisa Gullén in the Fine Arts School of Valencia explain why both artists consider that a solid artistic training and a knowledge of the history of art are essential parts of a designer's development. This approach to design from a perspective which is initially closer to the world of art than that of the techniques of production and of technical questions is what gives the products of these Valencian designers their freshness.

Figuerola and Gullén have a global vision of what constitutes design, analogous to the richness of their creative stimulants. Thus, they do not limit themselves to defining the product, its form, materials, finishes and productive methods, but see the design of the packaging and the graphics it carries as part of the process, rejecting the difference between graphic and industrial design.

Another important facet of the work of these Valencian designers is their compromise with environmental matters. For them, ecological design is a responsible answer to the crisis of natural resources and irreversible damage to the environment. Although it is not always possible to adopt strictly environmental criteria, which would in practise make their work impossible, they strive hard to find solutions within the existing productive system.

Figuerola and Gulléns's posture is completely clear in this respect: designers should assume their responsibilities, rejecting the use of materials or products which may do harm to the environment and trying to design objects that are long-lasting and have low production costs. •

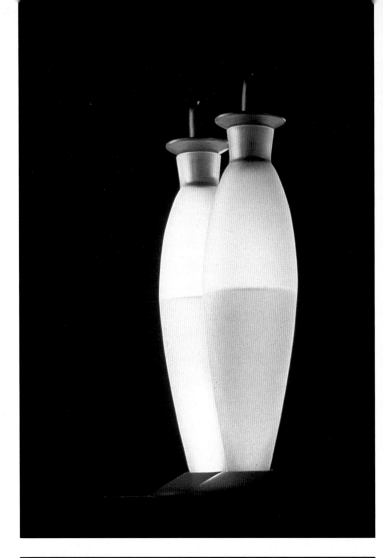

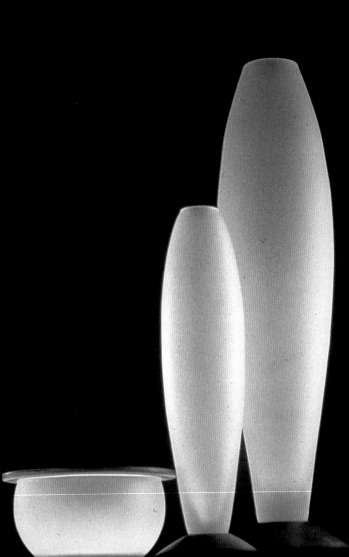

"Glauca" collection. Vinegar bottles made of ceramic and glass. The glass, 100% recycled, is molded by hand blowing and then handworked.

"Glauca" collection. Flower vases and ashtray. The glass is also 100% recycled and hand blown and the finish is achieved by high pressure sand-blasting.

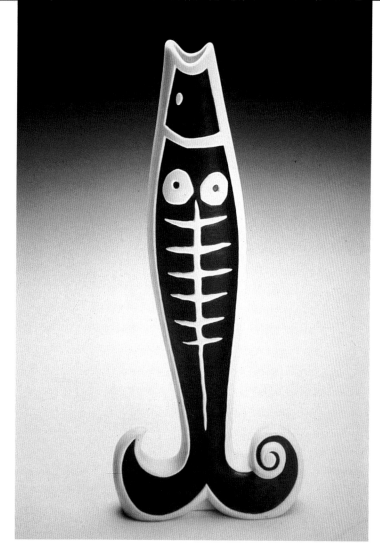

Fish-shaped flower vase (1990). A prototype made of porcelain.

"Devil" (1991) A stainless steel and porcelain serving bowl made for the Alessi company. The reference is to the rituals involved with serving and eating food, the Devil ironically representing the sin of gluttony.

Bed-linen from the "Oh!" collection made for Castilla Textil S.A. The sets of bed-linen are treated as spaces to represent life in bed. (1989)

"Matarile" Drawing room furniture. Prototype of veneered wood made expressly for the "Progetti e Territori" cultural exhibition which formed part of the "Abitare el Tempo" fair in Verona 1994.

"Goa" carpet, hand-woven of wool in India for Gandía Blasco.

*"Gertrudis" chair (1994)
Made for the cultural exhibition "Progetti e Territori" at the "Arbitare el Tempo"
fair in Verona.*

"Celeste" bedspread of cotton and linen, handmade and crocheted in India for Gandía Blasco. (1995)

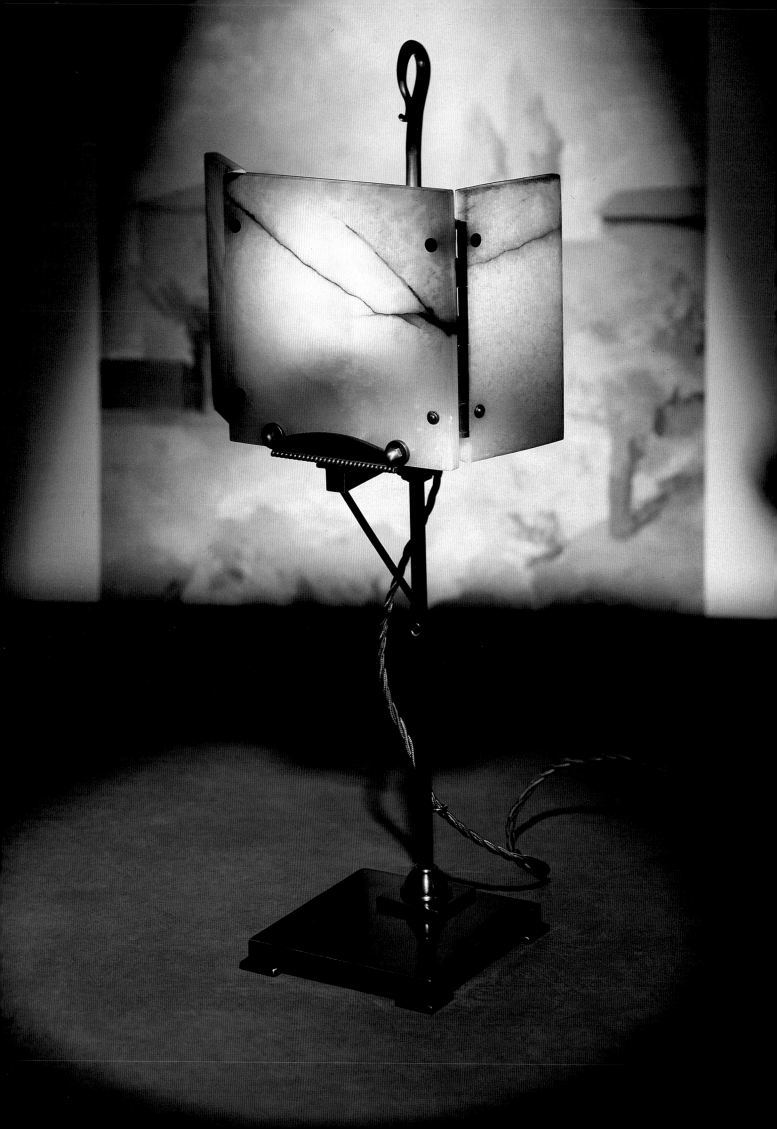

Michael Graves

Michael Graves, American by birth, is one of the most representative architects of the last few decades. In the seventies he was one of a group of five young independent architects (the others were Richard Meier, Peter Eisenman, John Hedjuk and Charles Gwathmey) known as the "White group" due to an exhibition in the M.O.M.A. of New York in 1969, who have dominated the architecture of the United States since that time. Graves's works, above all the Portland Building, constructed in1980, constitute a permanent reference to the post-modern movement of the last decade, together with the work of Leon Krier, Ricardo Bofill and Robert Stern.

Although the sixty people now working in Graves's firm are dedicated principally to architecture, the desire to achieve a unitary and complete design in all their projects has also led them to design furniture, cloth and artisanal pieces.

From large-scale urban projects to single detached houses to everyday objects, Michael Graves shows his ability to design in different registers for different projects, no matter what the size, always with one common feature: the figurative aspect.

Clock of maple and ebony for
Alessi. (1986)

Collection of resin bathroom objects for
"Projects" (1995)

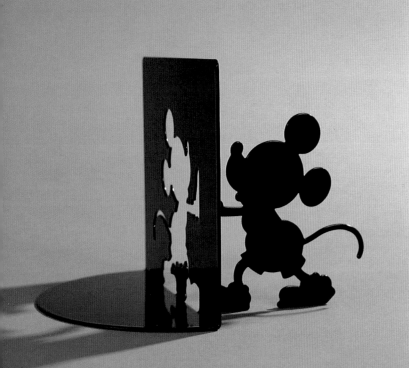

"Mickey & Co." (1994)
Bookend in enamelled steel. Produced
for Walt Disney and manufactured by
Moller Design.

Collection of cherry wood bookends
for Gilbert International (1992).

For Michael Graves, any projected design should be accessible, not only symbolically but also pragmatically, and therefore the emphasis is always on easy understanding on the part of the user.

Graves uses shapes and images which are well established in the public consciousness. They may be historic or artistic, such as his references to classical architecture, or commercial, like his products for Walt Disney. In this way, the incorporation of images foreign to the world of design and architecture suggest a lessening of the importance of the strict parameters which are the norm in these disciplines. In addition, in many of Graves's objects and buildings, there is a greater concern for the image than for function or space. This displacement of the architect's vision represents a recognition of the transformations suffered by society and of the way in which people relate to objects. On many occasions, the first contact with a piece of furniture or a building is through catalogues, magazines, books or even television.

Saltcellar and pepper grinder in
stainless steel for Alessi. (1987)

"Mickey Mouse Gourmet" Collection. (1993)
Teapot, sugar bowl and milk jar made of
stainless steel and heat-resistant plastic.
Produced for Walt Disney and manufactured
by Moller Design.

Teapot, sugar bowl and milk jar, also in
stainless steel and heat-resistant plastic for
Alessi. (1985)

His designs do not experiment with shapes,
feelings or materials unless they can be included
as part of a design that is understandable by
anyone, as for Graves the most important part
of any creative project is to establish a dialogue
directly with the consumer, without
cognitive limitations. ●

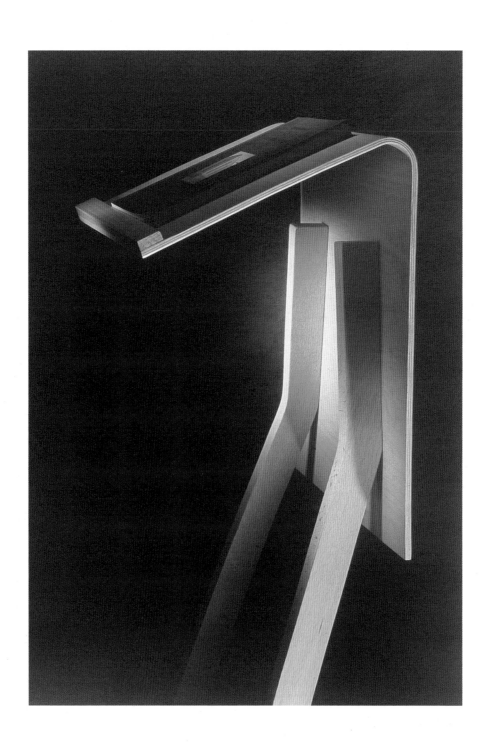

There are designers who try to find uses for objects that do not yet exist and others who imagine more or less complex new forms for already existing uses, but others simply try to provide improved solutions to old problems, without the final image of the product being of primordial importance. The objects presented here, designed by Konstantin Grcic, fall into the third category. Neither the "Step" library ladder, nor the "KGB" extendable table attempt anything more than a pure shape and a resolution of the problems that other designs have left unsolved.

"Step" takes a new look at the library ladder. These first appeared in English libraries halfway through the eighteenth century, and were considered useful but somewhat strange objects which were almost always hidden from sight. For this reason they were often camouflaged to appear as other types of furniture, from seats and stools to desks and tables.

This type of stairs appears to exist only when it is necessary, and so receives little attention most of the time. All that is asked of them is that they perform their function correctly and safely.

It may then seem unnecessary to go back and think again about something that is so defined

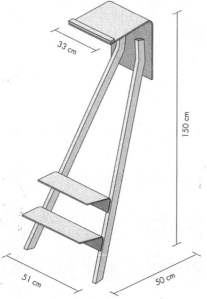

The two steps allow a reach of up to 2.5 metres. The ladder can be supported against any type of library shelving.

Its manageable dimensions and weight (9kg) mean that "Step" is easily moved.

62

KGB *(1994).*
Production: Nils
Holger Moorman.
Extendable table.

KGB : a metal structure,
with a linoleum surface and
wooden sides which support
the extending leaves, thus
avoiding scratching the
table-top.

and anonymous, but a good design has, at times, the capacity to throw new light on something that seems obvious and lacking in interest. "Step" has this capacity. It is not just an accessory added to the bookshelves, but, without wheels or rails, it leans into and is supported by the shelves. The small surface designed to allow books to be read without descending the stairs has a lower edge that permits the stairs to be hung up when not in use.

The "KGB" table analogously treats an already existing idea – the folding table – and by a small but incisive variation improves it. The traditional extension mechanism, which originated in Holland - two leaves which slide along rails concealed by the table-top – resulted in various problems. The rails became obstructed, the leaves banged against each other, the moving parts stuck, the central panel fell into place too heavily, and there was always the risk of fingers getting caught somewhere. Grcic analysed the principles of the system, noted their faults, and proposed a new design with the laudable intention of solving them, no small task. •

Porcelain table service (1995)
Designed for Royal Copenhagen A/S.

Ole Jensen

"The big department stores and shops which open until late on Saturdays are not in business to answer peoples needs or to provide things more cheaply. Perhaps all they do is take away peoples leisure time. They have been conceived to sell products which in reality are not necessary at all, but are promoted as bargains and this is one type of thinking that people really do not need.

There is only one thing that a designer should not consider as his job: selling the product. On the contrary, the tasks of design and selling should be seperated in order to best use the talents and qualities of all those involved in the process.

Equally, when you try to design something you realize that design is not just something amusing. Everything has its opposite: fun and seriousness, liberty and laws. If you realize this, as a designer, you discover for the same reason, that the work is never just boring or serious, but also optimistic.

Design is more than a cake or a happy wedding party. It is also Vitamin C and doing the dishes.

Designs in the future will be created by groups of specialists. Quality is not something which is sold. It is something which is given.

Deciding to do something new at any cost is

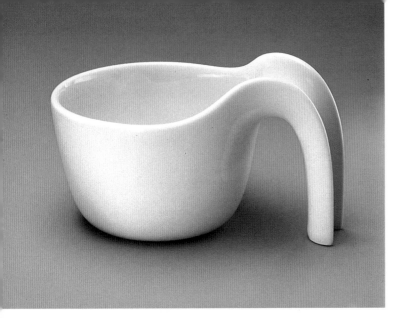

Porcelain cup. (1995)
Designed for Royal Copenhagen A/S.

Earthenware teapot. (1993)
Made for the furniture firm Paustian
A/S, Copenhagen.

Earthenware colander for Royal
Copenhagen A/S. (1995)

Earthenware juice jug for Royal
Copenhagen. (1995)

both impossible and unhealthy. Instead of taking novelty as the starting point, a designer should investigate things in depth and then establish the foundations for something new to happen.

Potatoes, carrots and oranges have a determined shape and are what they always were, just like water, coffee and milk are still amorphous liquids. These phenomena are in fact your only invariable limitations when trying to develop utensils for everyday eating.

It's banal, but an understanding of these primary rules is a precondition for an in-depth investigation into how things work. As far as possible it is the right and the duty of the designer to re-think things. In my opinion, materials, the same as potatoes and oranges, have their own nature, which is far from being utilized optimally by industrial methods. In all my designs I try to include natural phenomena as partners in the game, and not as something that needs to be counteracted. In this way, the designer becomes part of a larger whole."●

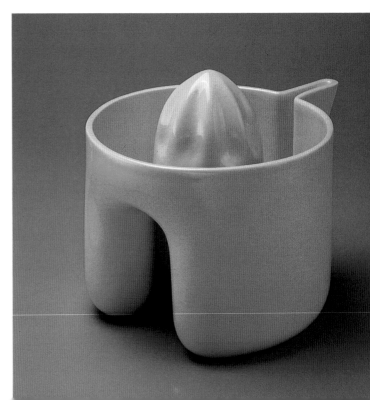

Stone jug. (1986)
A one-off piece designed for the
porcelain company Bing & Grondahl
A/S, Copenhagen.

Receptacles to wash the dishes in
(1996)
Made of sheets of vulcanized
rubber. The red rubber is natural,
the black synthetic.

Receptacle and brush. (1996)
Receptacle of soft rubber with sewn
edges and a brush made of beechwood
with pigs hair bristles.

Axel Kufus

The designs of Axel Kufus are based on four premises: the creation of an easily and cheaply produced modular system, effective storage in a small space, easy assembly for people without special knowledge or tools, and finally, a versatile system that means the modules can be used in many combinations.

All these have led to a design in which function is the guiding word and there are no gratuitous aesthetic features. A transparent design defined by the method of assembly, which is economic not only in the use of material but also in the effort needed to assemble the system and, as a result, in its form.

Kufus takes purity of form to the limit, minimizing the shape until all that remains is what is strictly necessary for the object to function. There are only two concessions: a constant geometrical rigidity, and an exhaustive concern for proportion, which is what, in the final instance, gives his designs their character.

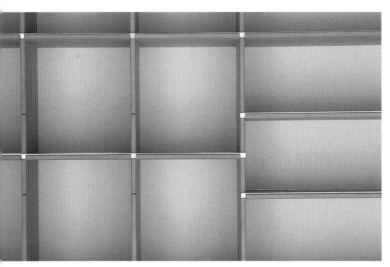

A standardized modular system allows the individual user to decide the dimensions and final configuration of the shelves according to personal needs.

In 1991, the "FNP" shelving system received the "Design Innovations" prize from the Design Zentrum of Nordrhein Westfalen.

"Lader" (1995). Production: Nils Holger Moormann. A system of drawers in plywood faced with birch.

The "Lader" system is composed of drawers of different capacities which may be freely grouped together. More modules can be added horizontally without the need to duplicate the side panels.

Herbert Ludwikowski

A common problem for many designers is having their designs accepted by the companies that control the market, who generally do not take risks and stick to what is known to be commercially acceptable. Herbert Ludwikowski was no exception, and for this reason, in 1985, he started production of his own designs, which were later accepted by various international companies. By this type of temporary agreement he has succeded in distributing his works firstly in important cities such as Frankfurt, Cologne, Milan and New York, and later in wider markets such as the Asian Rim zone, where his products are increasingly appreciated for their conceptual clarity and their geometric simplicity. One of Herbert Ludwikowski's major concerns is controlling not only the design of each piece but also the manufacturing process and the presentation of the objects. To this end, he has recently opened his own showroom in Hanover, a space dedicated exclusively to his own production.

Ludwikowski considers that his furniture of

"Calypso" cupboard (1994)
Production: Solo Möbel.
The body is made of beechwood
or metallic laminate with a
coating of steel.

This cupboard is constructed
on the same principle as the
"Swing" mirror. It can turn on
its axis and may be affixed
either to the wall or between
floor and ceiling.

minimal lines is a reaction to the ever more complex technologies and overwhelming number of stimuli of modern society. His pieces, based on the principle "less is more" formulated by the German architect Mies van de Rohe, confide in the purity of form and the transparency of ideas to ensure that their integration with any surroundings is possible. This effort to simplify the object comes not so much from a concern for space, cost, or the simplification of manufacturing systems as from a wish to liberate the piece from the necessity of having an associated spatial context. For this reason, one of the most distinguishing characteristics of the pieces of Herbert Ludwikowski, one which makes it really different, is the enormous autonomy which the German designer has been capable of giving them. When we analyse the "Swing" mirror or the "Calypso" wardrobe, what calls our attention insistently is the impression that they do not belong to any specific space and are not linked to any particular room, but could be installed in the

The component pieces of "Calypso" are interchangeable, which means they can be used for diverse purposes.

"Calypso" offers the possibility of incorporating a full-length mirror on one side. The shelves may be of glass, beechwood or steel laminate.

"Tutto" (1989)
Production: Solo Möbel.
A shelving system also affixable to the
wall or to the floor and ceiling. The
structure is of matt or polished chrome
and the shelves of sand-blasted glass.

The width of the "Tutto" system
is variable depending on the
shelves used.

hall, the bedroom, living room, bathroom or even the passageway. Both pieces of furniture have gyratory supports of metal tubing. This shows that they are not designed to be placed against walls but rather away from them. The mechanism which permits them to turn on a vertical axis, as well as making their use possible from different positions, means it is necessary to create an empty space around them, emphasizing their condition of solitary objects.

Likewise, the various objects for the bathroom, "Taifun", "Captain Cook" and "America's cup" give the impression that they could be found as easily in a dressing room, a bedroom or a hall, as in the bathroom. The designer has given them a feeling of extreme lightness and an image of fortuitousness, not only in relation to their own presence but also in concordance with the dialogue that is established with the user. For these reasons, the simplification of form and the minimization of the object do not constitute an extreme distillation of the strictly functional, but just the opposite. One could say that Herbert Ludwikowski, through his objects, liberates space from the imprint of the functional. He entraps function in his minimal and autonomous furniture, leaving them like sculptures, and

"Captain Cook" (1989)
Production: Solo Möbel.
A combination of shelves and auxiliary
table designed for small kitchens. The
table folds down when not needed, and
the shelves are pivoted.

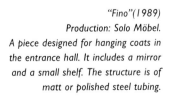

"Fino"(1989)
Production: Solo Möbel.
A piece designed for hanging coats in
the entrance hall. It includes a mirror
and a small shelf. The structure is of
matt or polished steel tubing.

empties space of any immediate meaning. In this manner he succeeds in not conditioning the room with his objects, and leaves them empty to be filled only by a human presence.

In addition, although each piece is designed to stand alone, Herbert Ludwikowski's furniture forms part of a modular system which allows it to be combined, thus offering multiple possibilities modifiable according to the needs of the user. However, this flexible and modular idea of the object does not imply that they can be easily erected by the user. On the contrary, the pure shapes of the pieces are complemented by the extraordinary quality of the finishes, which requires great care to be taken during their installation.●

"Laser" (1989)
Production: Solo Möbel.
The two steel tubes which comprise this piece are affixed to the wall and support all the other components: light, shelves, towel-rack and mirrors. The washbasin is designed and produced by Rapsel.

"Taifun" (1986)
is a structure of steel tubing designed for the bathroom and produced by Solo Möbel. The "Euclide" washbasin is developed and produced by Rapsel.

"America's cup" (1992)
Production: Solo Möbel.
A bathroom unit which includes a
free-standing washbasin, shelving and
mirror, all made of polished stainless
steel and glass.

Vico Magistretti

The long professional career of the architect Vico Magistretti is full of clues as to the way he approaches design. If we look at the Gaudi (1969) and Selene (1970) chairs, we can discover in their nakedness, his overriding concern to define the object with its own structure, which determines both the stability and rigidity of the piece as well as its comfort.

In his most recent work, which obeys different aesthetic and social postulates, the structure is no longer the flesh and bones of the object, but rather a covered, although not hidden, skeleton.

The designs on the following pages show, with the clarity of an X-ray, what is behind their appearance, as the philosphy with which they were conceived leaves no room for doubt. What we see here is not an aprioristic desire, but an honesty with respect to the very act of thinking that is transmitted to the objects and makes the designs eminently trustworthy, and in all probability, something long-lasting.

Vico Magistretti recommends that young designers never try to design things on a large scale such as 2:1 or 3:1. The important thing is

"Chaise" (1996)
Produced by é De Padova.
Chairs with sinuous lines mounted
on small wheels which make them
easy to move.

"Chaise Longue" (1996)
Produced by é De Padova.
A variation of the "Chaise" chairs,
with a seat that is lengthened
sufficiently to recline on.

Variants (1996)
Produced by é De Padova.
A collection of sofas and armchair with
an aluminium structure covered in
polyurethane.

the concept. "The artisan will know a hundred times better than you how to settle things. All you have to understand is the way in which they are made, to know the dynamic of the forces." This sentence reveals not only the conceptual character of Magistretti's designs, but also his gift. He conceives his profession as a continuous dialogue between all parts involved, the producer, the artisan and the user. He is not so concerned with controlling each and every one of the stages of production of his objects but rather with shedding light on the essential ideas.

Magistretti abhors details. If the design is correct, the detail should already be included in the overall concept of the object. Detail understood as the anecdotic is an error. What is really essential can not be settled by an appendix or by an added piece, and in contrast, it makes no sense for what is unnecessary to appear as some kind of parasitical addition.

One of the mistakes that could be made when trying to analyse the work of Vico Magistretti is trying to associate it with a particular artistic current or fashion, or some type of "-ism".

Some have attempted to see in Magistretti's work an anticipation of minimalism. Perhaps when we look at the "Serbelloni" or "Incisa" chairs, it is possible to recognize some similarities with the post-war work of Eames. However, these chairs were designed between 1992 and 1994.

"Serbelloni" (1994) – "Incisa" (1992)
Produced by é De Padova.
The polyurethane is covered on the exterior
with leather, while the interior covering, of
leather or cloth, can be unzipped and
removed.

The difference between the two
chairs lies in the form of the feet and
the fact that the "Serbelloni" is
height-adjustable (right photo). Both
chairs are rotating.

Any references in the work of Victor Magistretti
are nothing more than imprecise parallels, with
which it would be possible to reconstruct the entire
history of design in the second half of the century.
The influences are echoes, voices that surround a
trajectory with an extraordinary internal coherence.
This does not mean that it is a strictly homogenous
trajectory, but what does not change is his spirit,
his way of understanding the designers job. The
changes, the variation of themes, overcoming of
some preoccupations and the appearance of others,
are nothing more than the logical evolution
necessary to such an extensive career.

Borges has said that the work of some authors
merited anonymity. The Argentine author

Louisiana (1993) Produced by é De Padova.
A chair whose seat is constructed in a way
similar to the "Serbelloni" and "Incisa". The chair
rests on four small wheels which minimize the
legs. The design includes a pouffe.

"Shine" (1995).
Manufactured by é De Padova.
A piece made from plywood faced with
cherry or spruce. The face of the
drawers is of anodized aluminium with
a silver satinized finish.

"Babe III" (1988)
Produced by é De Padova.
An oval folding table whose structure is
made of cherrywood with a top made of
two layers of plywood treated with special
resin and polyurethane pigment varnishes,
or of cherrywood treated with aniline dyes.

"Vidum" (1987)
Produced by é De Padova.
A table with a circular or rectangular glass
top. The base is composed of three wooden
legs made of natural beechwood, painted or
aniline dyed, which allow the height to be
regulated using a wooden screw.

"Shine" (1991) Manufactured by
é De Padova.
A table with an aluminium
structure and a surface of cherry
or spruce wood or white laminate.

"Shigeto" (1989) Produced by
é De Padova.
A cupboard with two doors made of
plywood faced with American cherrywood
with aniline dyes, mounted on wheels.
The front wheels have a braking system.

considered anonymity a privilege. The meaning of classicism in its purest sense is that the image of the work persists in the collective memory without the author being remembered. In the sphere of industrial design this also occurs at times. Certain pieces seem to have an immediacy that makes it seem they were never "designed" as such. However, when this happens with objects as recent as the latest designs of Vico Magistretti, this implies an enormous exercise of humility and rigour. ●

*"Tani Moto" (1991) Produced by
é De Padova.
Cabinet with glass doors and a
frame of solid beechwood.*

*"Tani Moto" (1991)
Produced by é De Padova.
A bookcase based on the same
idea and structure as the
cabinet in the picture above.
The shelves are of plywood
faced with beechwood or
painted white.*

Peter Maly

"The intention was to produce a system of minimalist furniture of extreme simplicity and linear clarity.» The words of the designer Peter Maly, explaining his ideas for the Duo shelving system, clearly define his approach to the project.

"Duo" is a system of shelves and containers strongly based on logic and versatility, in which clarity of composition is the guide-line. The "Duo" system is a good example of a design conceived from a neutral point of view, which proposes nothing more than that it be useful, timeless and easily accepted by the user, and that

in this form the objects can be located in any surroundings. Perhaps the most significant element of the Duo system is the disk-shaped coupling which joins the different modules of the system. Thanks to this coupling, each piece can be set on angle completely different from the others. This means that the configuration could be completely aligned or forming a straight angle in a corner or adapted to a difficult corner with another type of angle or even in an irregular line that could be used to divide a room into two different atmospheres. The modules could even

"Duo" containers. Production: Interlübke.
The modules are available in two widths,
77.5cm and 150cm, allowing various
possibilities. The joints between the
modules are rotating so that the pieces
can be arranged in different ways to
create differing spaces in the same room.

Container and table from the "Duo" system.
"Duo" also allows the containers to be arranged
individually. The interior arrangement of the shelving
also permits various combinations.

Shelves and hi-fi stand. "Duo" system.
Production: Interlübke.
Upper cupboards of painted aluminium.
Shelves and drawers of beechwood.

The open combination between the
upper cupboards and the shelves of
various lengths allows the free
creation of images.

fold in on themselves completely, thus closing the shelves. This flexibility in the overall concept of the system is also apparent in the design of the shelves and drawers, which permits multiple combinations.

However, there is no wish on the part of the designer to leave his mark on the objects, to ensure that his name is embedded in the material. On the contrary, Maly tries to create objects that simply by their use, their optimally used materials, and their purity of form which leave no space for rhetoric, are transformed into classic, timeless pieces. •

Angelo Mangiarotti

Angelo Mangiarotti has, throughout his professional trajectory, combined his work as a designer with an intellectual and theoretical vision of design. Only five years after graduating as an architect from the University of Milan in 1948, he was invited to become a teacher in the I.T.T. of Chicago. His academic activities have led him to various universities Adelaide, Hawaii, Lausanne, Milan and to appear in numerous publications magazines, books and newspapers. This activity is not something parallel to his work as a designer and architect, on the contrary, this intellectual vision has conditioned all his works,

leaving an indelible mark on them.

The designs of this Italian architect are characterised by an attempt to show the intrinsic qualities of each object, both in architecture proper, and in industrial design.

According to Mangiarotti, only an "objective" design can avoid diverting the user from the essence of the object which transforms it into something collectively recognisable, going beyond the entity of the particular designer.

This objectivity is, for Mangiarotti, the expression of the characteristics of the materials and of the techniques used, and through them,

"Kyathos" (1987)
Glass vase produced for
Cristaleria Colle.

"Caffettiera" (1990).
Steel and aluminium coffee pot, for Mepra.

looking for a new relationship between man and his surroundings, between man and the object.

Thus, the objects of glass, aluminium or plastic claim the original liquid qualities of their materials: the glass objects express not only their obvious transparency, but, through their slightly inclined sinuous shapes remind us that at some time they were something as liquid as the water they contain; the aluminium coffee pot is deformed and distorted, reminding us of the high temperatures of the oven where it was formed; the pieces of aluminium cutlery seem to retain a certain plasticity that modifies their lines. ●

"Olpe" (1987)
Glass oil container designed for
Cristaleria Colle.

98

"Ergonomica series". Steel cutlery. (1990)
This collection of objects for dining was designed for Mepra following ergonomic criteria.

"Ergonomica series".
Sauce container. (1990)
The "Ergonomica" collection received the Plus prize in 1991.

"Dumbo"(1996).
Diffusing lamp produced for Disano.
The form of the objects designed by Mangiarotti emphasizes the intrinsic characteristics of the materials used. For this Italian architect, it is essential to display the plasticity of plastic materials and the fluidity of liquids.

Javier Mariscal

"I'm not a designer who provides mechanical, functional solutions like an engineer. I provide something else, messages of colour, objects I try to imbue with poetry and philosophy in order to claim a different way of thinking and living".

Throughout his career, Javier Mariscal's curiosity has led him to explore things from all angles, without limiting himself to any particular design field. His work includes comics, animations, paintings, sculpture and graphic, industrial and interior design, in all of which fields his creative bent is more than evident. The dividing line between one activity and another are not clear. Mariscal mixes them on purpose. He contaminates design with the aesthetic of the comic and vice-versa. From this singular position, based not only on his coming from the field of comic drawing, but also on his continuing to combine both facets without establishing any clear hierachy, there is a clear benefit to all his work.

His way of doing things is festive, playful and natural, and is consistent with an uncommon candor without the least pretence of purity, and he has successfully translated this spirit from his

colourful comics to the field of industrial design.

Mariscal's products are enjoyable, because he himself seems to enjoy creating them. In his objects one sees a capacity for surprise, for play, for seeing and touching life, all without any limitation or preconception, as he himself says: "Many things inspire me. There is no difference between a Goya painting, a good television programme, an advert, a theatrical play, a comic or a Ferris wheel. All of them can be equally inspiring. I don't believe that one form of art is better or worse than another."

Javier Mariscal's iconoclastic and uninhibited approach has exceeded his own objectives and has become a dissonant opinion within the world of design. In a relatively new profession with a certain tendency to self-affirmation and to imbuing any action with excessive gravity, the frivolous attitude of Mariscal is unusual. •

"Alessandra" (1995-1996)
Another chair from the collection "Los muebles amorosos".

The design of this collection of chairs and sofas is a restatement of Mariscal´s work in other fields, the three dimensions of the seats using the shapes and colours of his previous work in two dimensions.

"Saula marina" (1995-1996) Produced by Moroso.
A sofa with sinuous lines and ingeniously designed fabrics from the collection "Los muebles amorosos".

The collection "Los meubles amorosos" was designed by Javier Mariscal in collaboration with the architect Ron Arad.

"León solitario" (1994)
Wool carpet, dimensions 170 x 240cm, belonging
to the same collection as "Quiero estar en tu casa",
produced by Nani Marquina.

"Quiero estar en tu casa" (1994)
Wool carpet, dimensions 170 x 240cm, produced by
Nani Marquina. Handtufted in India.

Model "Por la mitad" (1994)
Dimensions: 170 x 240cm.
100% wool carpets, handtufted in India.

Nani Marquina

Nani Marquina studied industrial design in the Escuela Massana of Barcelona. His professional experience started with interior design projects, which were followed by a period dedicated to textile design in collaboration with various companies. In 1986, he created his own company producing designs for carpets, cloth, and textile accessories.

His early experience in interior decoration has meant that his subsequent work has shown a special sensitivity to materials and colours and their relationship with their surroundings.

The carpets which are shown here, produced by his own company, reflect this concern for the interior space, rudimentarily comfortable, in which the object is situated. The carpets radiate warmth, and a great part of their attractiveness is that they seem to have been designed especially to hang on walls. The idea of a carpet that can be looked at like a painting also helps to break down traditional notions of floor coverings.

These pieces by Marquina lead us to reconsider our notions of the horizontal plane the floor, and the vertical one the walls.

MIS CARICIAS
SON COSQUILLAS
SON COSQUILLAS
MIS CARICIAS
MIS CARICIAS
SON COSQUILLAS
SON COSQUILLAS
MIS CARICIAS
MIS CARICIAS
SON COSQUILLAS

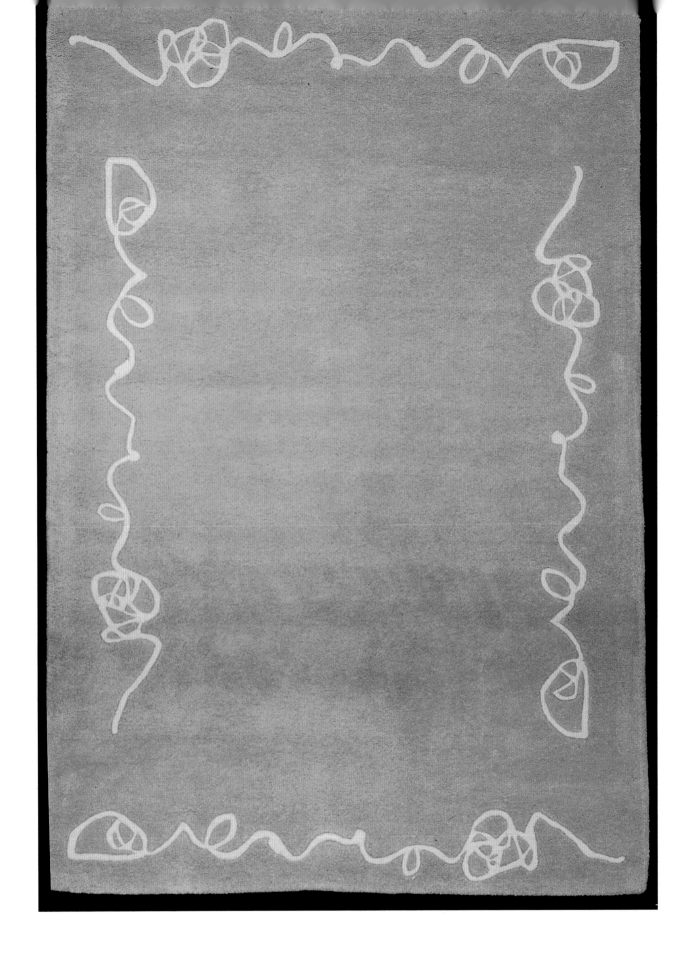

Model " Palabras" (1995)
Dimensions: 170 x 240cm.

Model "Alambre" (1996)
Dimensions: 170 x 240cm.

Model "Begonia". (1989)
Dimensions: 200 x 260cm.

Model "Doce." (1984)
Dimensions: 170 x 240cm.

Clay models. Objects designed between
1988-1993.

Ursula Munch-Petersen

Working in an artisanally fashion produces a loving relationship with the material in question which is clearly reflected in the models made. The design process after this stage can be considered a persistence and a protection of the first idea, at the same time as one is collaborating with productive and economic conditions.

The modelling stage is characterized by curiosity and interest, a state of innocence with a multitude of possibilities and a high degree of uncertainty as to whether the idea is ugly or beautiful, as if one was on a desert island, where everything had to be thought out from new.

A fountain is a cavity where rain accumulates, a cup is a mixture of a spoon, a saucepan and a pot which contains the quantiy that is drunk at any one time. We are so inundated by domestic objects that it is difficult to discern and comprehend their functions in any sense but the conventional.

The original reason for using varnish was to give the clay a smooth and impervious surface. However, the similarity of varnish to running water, both in the artisanal stage and in the finished work, means that the pottery can be seen as petrified images of the ocean and the earth

giving us the possibility of working with tiny models of the universe in our studios.

In addition to the solitary experimentation by artists with respect to possibilities and limitations, it would be a good thing to prolong the atmosphere of the design school, where a whole group of people are dedicated to the same task and the objects are presented as words in a conversation, with the communication being produced by means of the material and the form. Exhibitions are partly a type of slow communication where artists leave messages for their colleagues.

In our time, the influence of concepts such as efficacy, sales and economics is enormous. As an artisan/designer, our work tries to give wider meaning to daily spaces."•

Ursula Munch-Petersen

*Table objects produced for Royal
Copenhagen. (1992)*

André Ricard

"I like to compare the designer to an actor. We don't write the script, but we interpret it. I think the best actors are those who can put themselves into the skin of a new personality and are not always the same. I try to adapt myself substantially to what is asked of me, depending on the client and on the subject, and to let myself disappear a little, although naturally, this is difficult and your self is always present to some degree"

In André Ricard, there exists this wish for anonymity. Perhaps because for some time he has been designing perfume bottles, he has developed a certain protean quality, taking on a different personality in each case, for each new design, related with the image of the product or the identity of the client. In any case, it is a transformation that only affects the superficial aspects of the objects, and not the mechanisms of designing. Ricard's way of working is always methodic and rigorous.

For Ricard, the anonymity of the designer constitutes one of the qualities of the product. Objects must conform to their own laws, which have little to do with trends in fashion or flashy inspiration or with the caprices of the author. "To link fashion and design seems ridiculous to me.

"Ferro" carpet in 100% wool. (1991)
Dimensions: 200 x 260cm.
According to André Ricard, the pattern of this carpet is inspired by the idea of electricity pylons whose framework of metal structures is an aesthetic for our time.

"Drac" chair. (1991)

A light chair composed of two linked arcs supporting the seat. One of them extends to form the arm and fix the back.

Structural plan of the components.

Aluminium structure forged at low pressure. The seat and arm-back rest are of semi-rigid injected polyurathane covered in leather.

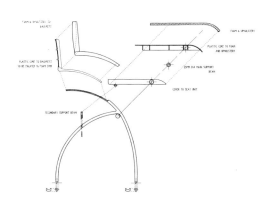

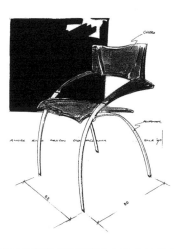

Salt-cellar designed for Nani Marquina. (1992)

Shower head designed for Ta-Tay S.A. plastics (1994)

Shower made of injected plastic. Attention has been paid to the angle where the handle and the head meet in order to improve the ergonomic aspect, particularly with respect to washing the back.

The glass body which is slotted over the sides ensures a good grip when using the object.

The lateral perforations for the salt in the upper part and an aluminium lid in the base complete the details of the piece.

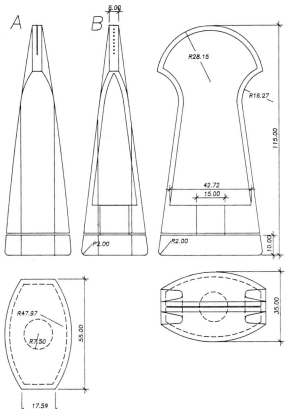

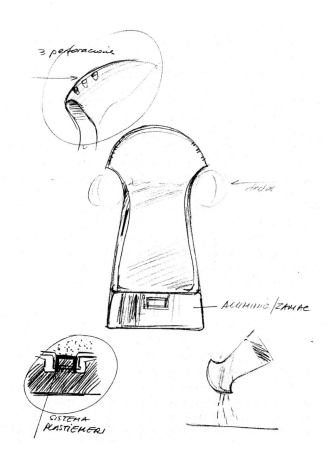

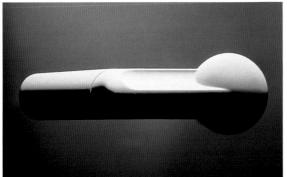

Fashion, as Cocteau said is "what goes out of fashion", what is by its own nature born converted into the past. In design, a well-resolved chair lives longer than the designer.

The work of André Ricard is an excellent example of design applied to everyday things. It is an attempt to influence the methods of production directly and to ensure that from the beginning, the products thus obtained take into account other factors than the all-powerful profit motive. In sum, without mortgaging the profitability of the product with superfluous aesthetic features there is an attempt to analyse the use of the object in question, the materials available and the methodology of the production process, in order to achieve a clear objective: improve the quality of life.

The long professional career of this industrial designer which includes collaborations with the most diverse type of companies including Amat furniture, Antonio Puig perfumes, BD design books, La Caixa savings bank, the International Olympic Committee, Fichet keys, Moulinex electrical goods, and Paco Rabanne, gives a good idea of his versatility and of his philosophy that any activity or product is susceptible to improvement by means of hard work and thought.●

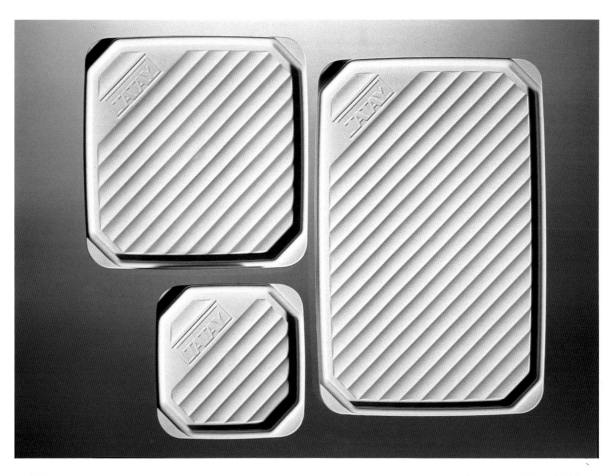

122

Food containers produced for
Ta-Tay S.A. plastics. (1994)

Four transparent chamfers in the
corners of the box allow the contents
to be seen.

The different sizes available are designed
for better use of space in the refrigerator.

The lid, grooved for greater rigidity, has
four tabs for opening from any side.

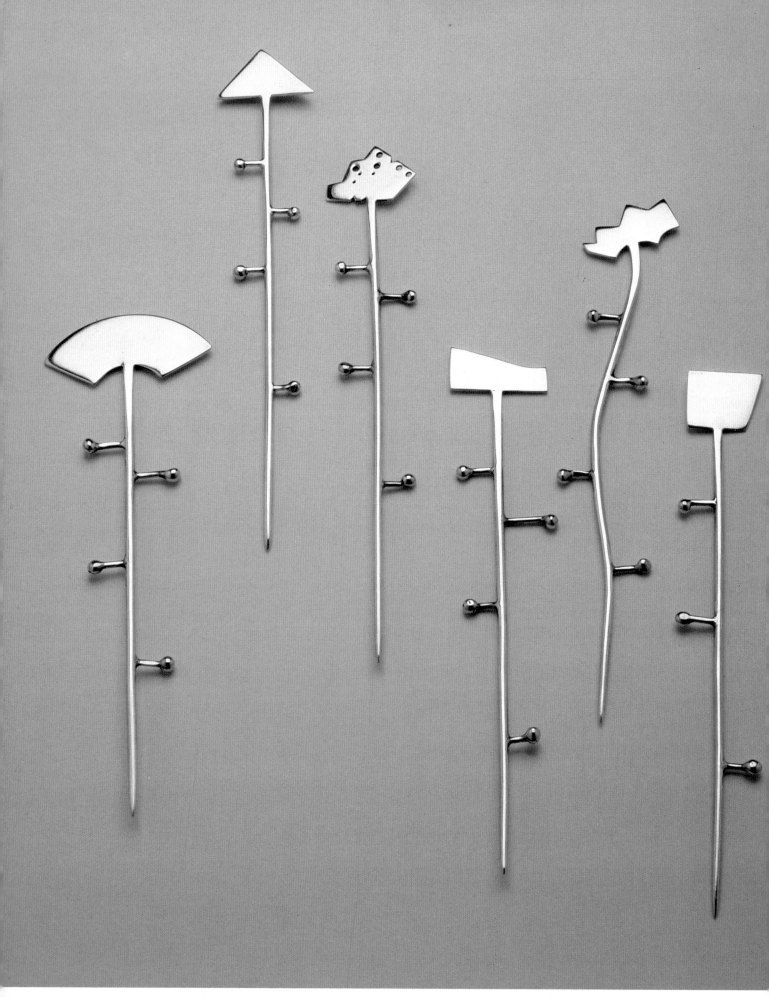
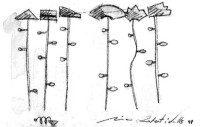

Núria Robert

The pieces made by Núria Robert speak of a different scale for household objects. These are not furniture or lamps, but small scale objects whose daily use means that often they do not receive the careful design accorded to them here.

Salt-cellars, letter openers, teaspoons, table lamps, items for the dressing-table, cocktail sticks and eraser holders are all treated like pieces of jewellery. Sprinkling salt or putting sugar in coffee cease to be automatic actions because the designs of Robert make the user aware of what they are doing.

In these almost jewel-like pieces, the visual dimension is amplified. The objects have shapes which make them different from their analogues, the same sort of thinking one might find in the design of a watch or a ring. At the same time, the objects shown here also show a concern for the tactile experience they may give. In short, the designs seem to accentuate the playful and personal aspects of the objects.

Silver spoon for the mouth of a
newly born baby. (1995)

Silver coffee spoons. (1992)

When one studies the complete collection of
cocktail sticks produced by Robert, one observes
that although the general lines are the same, there
are small differences between each piece. This
singularity gives them a certain mystery: two
things designed by the same person at the same
time, with the same function, made of the same
materials and with an almost identical shape,
nevertheless are imbued with a distinctive touch.
This is an uncompromising position with respect
to the logic of industrial production. The cocktail
sticks have a certain similarity to the prehistoric
artefacts found in archeological museums. Like
them, each one has been conceived as a singular
object. These coincidences transfigure the
impression we have of them. Due to their
similarity, they seem to result from a different

126

type of logic, one that comes to us with echoes of the ancient past.

Other objects, like the silver baby-spoon, may remind us of some of the sculptures of Joan Miró which use daily household utensils to construct human figures, utensils such as a water bucket, a plate or a rake. However, in this case the final meaning of these minimal sculptures is inverted. Instead of creating figures from spoons, the spoons are created from the figure. This does not produce a displacement of daily objects to the field of art, but rather an approximation of those images of contemporary art which are already taken for granted, and are thus recognizable, to the field of daily life. Something similar occurs with the salt and pepper pots: one could easily say that they belong to the chess set of Marcel Duchamp that appears in the famous photograph of Man Ray. As the shapes do not conform to the images associated with these types of objects, other images, of objects that do not have a strict

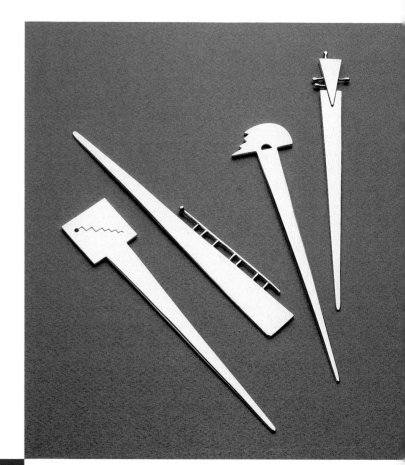

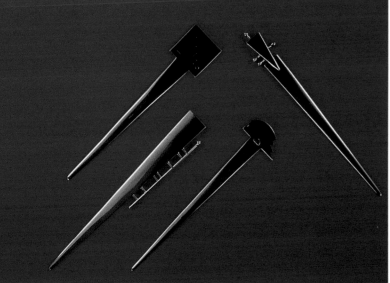

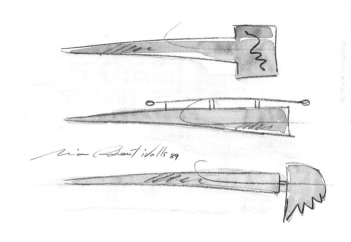

Silver letter openers. (1994)

function, such as sculptures, come immediately to mind. This does not mean for one moment that the objects were conceived on this basis. What is more, each observer will almost certainly have their own, different references. What is undoubtable is that Núria Robert manages to imbue her objects with a different meaning, one closely associated to art.

Marcel Duchamp moved a urinal from its natural setting to an exhibition room to convert it, in an ironical gesture, into a work of art. To convert the shape of a utensil into that of a sculture is surely a new variation on an old theme. •

Silver and rubber salt-and pepper-pots for the table. (1992)

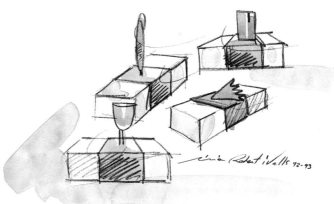

Silver eraser holder (1993)

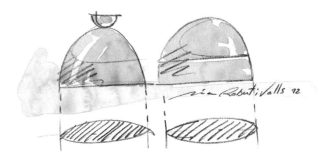

Perfume bottle and box for the
dressing-table. (1990)

130

Salt-cellar and pepper-pot (1995).
Produced for the Catalan College of Architects.
Materials: Oxidized bronze and silver.

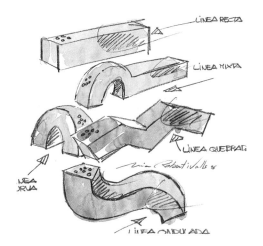

Table candlestick (1990).
Composed of a container for oil and a silver plate,
connected by a thread of the same material. The flattened
form was designed to break the verticality of the candle.

Franz Josef Schulte

Franz Josef Schulte first established his own design office in 1978 in the German city of Krefeld. During this first stage as an independent designer, he was producing designs for various companies, and it was not until 1991 that he set up his own company Schulte Design, so as to be able to control the whole process, including production.

The objects produced by Schulte are solid and monolithic, and although versatility is not their most obvious feature, they all have the possibility of change, of offering a certain variety in their look and use.

The "Fräulein M" chair can be changed by modifying some of the design components: the chair is of wood and the seat has either fixed upholstery or a slip-on cover that covers the back-rest as well. One of the singular aspects of this chair is that it is not constructed from the separate elements typical of a chair feet, seat and back rest but instead is based on the various planes afforded by single pieces of wood. Thus the

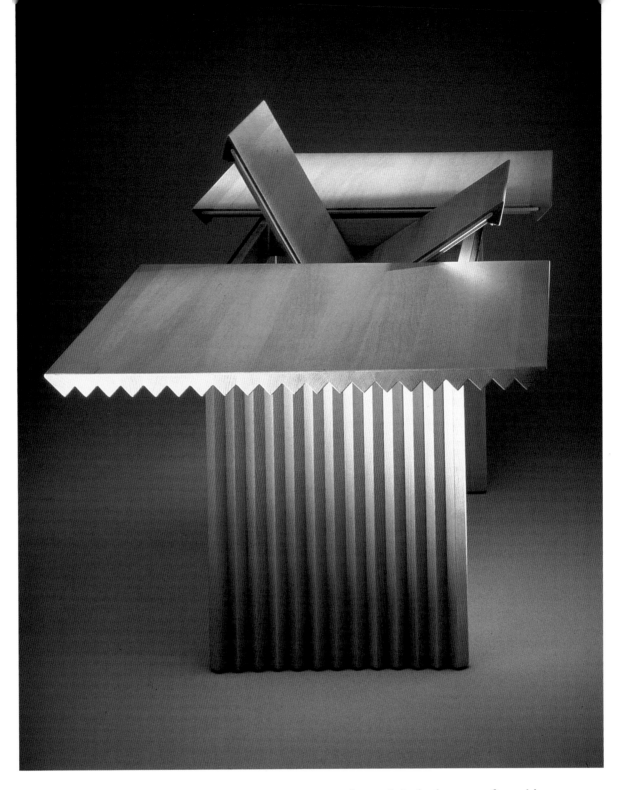

"Trian". Produced by Schulte Design.
A table made of beechwood for up to
six diners, which when extended can
accommodate ten.

rear feet and the back rest are formed by one
plane, the seat by another and the front feet by
another. The "Trian" table is extendable,
depending on the number of diners. The table top
is divided in the middle, so as to accommodate a
central section. The table has no legs, but instead
is supported by wooden panels. Both the
underside of the table top and the exterior of the
supports have a saw-tooth profile. This means that
although the thickness of the material is not very

great, the moment of inertia, and thus the capacity of resistance, are considerable.

Finally, the "Krefelder" wardrobe can be modified for various uses by altering the interior shelves and accessories. This piece of furniture has a base of 30 x 30cm and a height which varies between 120 and 143cm according to the model. It opens on one of the vertices and divides into two pieces which form right angles. The interior can be divided as wished into square or triangular trays, or tie-hangers, or sloping supports for shoes. ●

"Fräulein M" (1996). Produced by Schulte Design. A beechwood chair available in six colours.

Philippe Starck

In principle, the objectives which guide the designs of Philippe Starck are no different from those of any other designer. To know and give meaning to objects whatever size they may be (buildings, toothbrushes, chairs or lamps) and try to define a new relationship between man and materials, and above all, to make people happy.

What is special in Starck's designs is their genesis and the way in which he tries to carry out these objectives, that is, his contact with the world of dreams.

Starck's first approach to things is without doubt light-hearted and comes from his own particular dreamworld, and he succeeds in translating these ideas into concrete objects as if the productive process with all its restrictions did not exist. His objects seem to be the realization of dreams, dreams which appeal to the capacity for dreaming we all possess, and he tries to ensure that the relationship between object and user is thus more complex and enriching.

One cannot be indifferent to the designs of Starck. A diffuse line between reality and dreams means that either the suggestions thrown down are accepted or there is just no communication at all. •

"Faitoo"(1996). Produced for Alessi.
Cutlery, crockery and kitchen accessories designed together with a wall storage system.

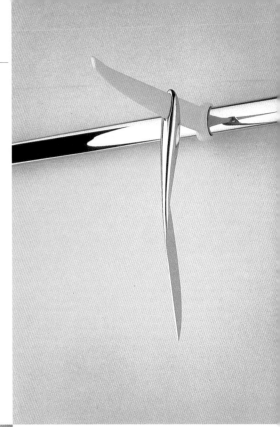

"Few of the objects designed by man have fulfilled their marvellous promise.
The "Faitoo" promise nothing, they are just for eating and drinking.
It's not much, but they try to do it honestly". (Philippe Starck)

Variation of the "Faitoo" system. Free-standing cutlery support.
The shapes of many of the objects designed by Starck bring to mind some of the sculptures at the first half of the century: Brancusi, Arp or Giacometti's surrealist period.

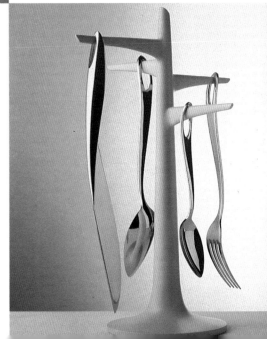

139

"Hot Berta" (1990-91). Production Alessi.
Kettle of aluminium coloured with silicone resins.
Handle and spout of polyamide.

"Ti Tang" (1992)
Production: Alessi
Teapot of white porcelain finished in
aluminium dyed grey with epoxy resins.

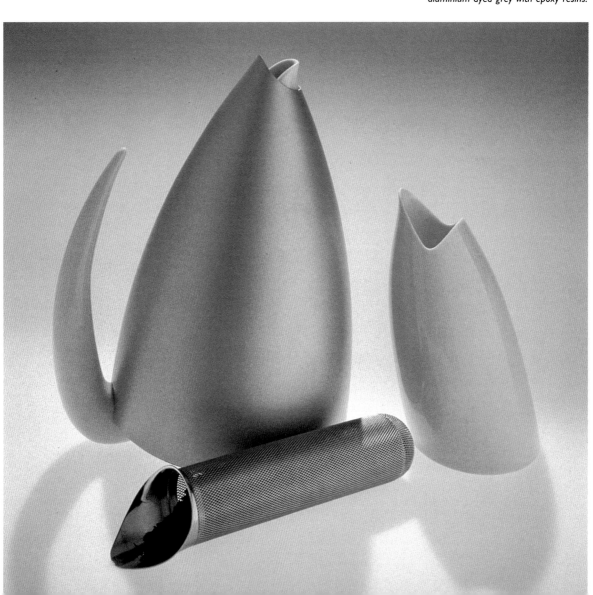

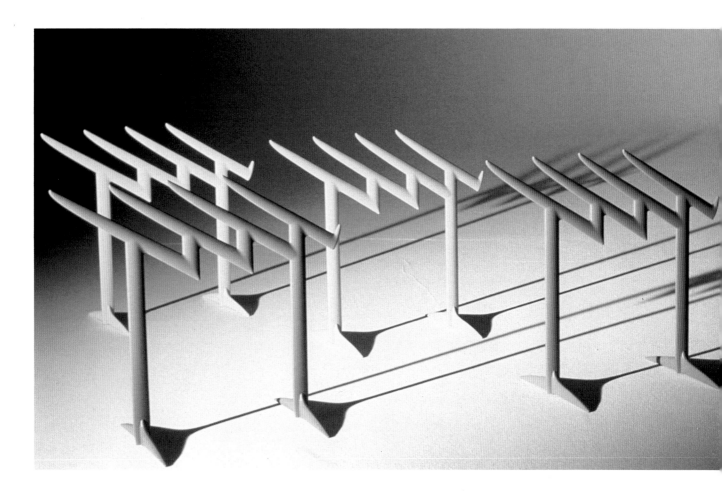

"Claudia Evangelista" (1996)
Produced for Kartell.
Magazine rack of high density
polystyrene.
Starck has baptized the magazine rack
with the names of the top models.

"Miss Trip" (1996)
Produced for Kartell.
Collapsible chair made of
polypropylene and beechwood, the first
time this combination of materials has
appeared on the market.
The chair, which can be completely
dismantled, is made of polypropylene
and beechwood, the first time this
combination of materials has appeared
on the market.
The back rest, made of planed beech,
attaches to the plastic seat. In the
same way, the turned beech legs are
coupled together using a specially
designed system.

*"Monsieur X".
Produced for XO.
Armchair, chaise-longue and
rocking chair, all with a collapsible
structure of natural or carob-dyed
beechwood, with the seat and
back of cotton in various colours.*

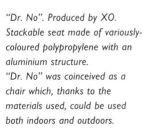

*"Dr. No". Produced by XO.
Stackable seat made of variously-
coloured polypropylene with an
aluminium structure.
"Dr. No" was coinceived as a
chair which, thanks to the
materials used, could be used
both indoors and outdoors.*

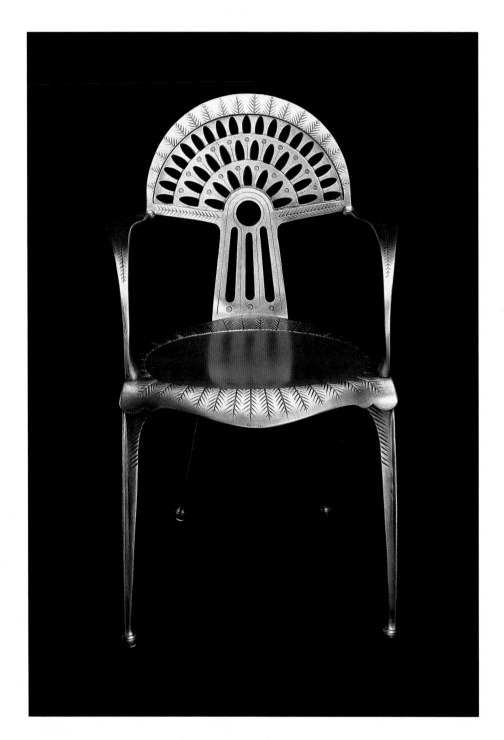

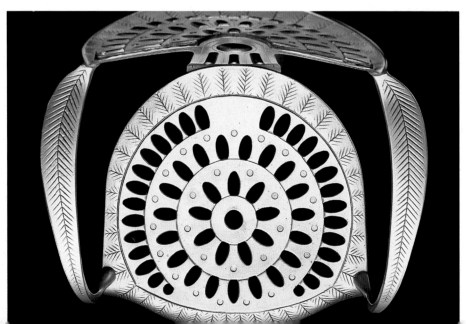

Norbert Wangen

The work of the designer Norbert Wangen is focused on the spatial investigation of structures which from a static point of view search for new solutions.

An example is the Attila folding seat, which can be reduced to a bi-dimensional panel, and came about as a result of research into the spatial possibilties of folding planes, using the same principle as a piece of paper trimmed to make shapes. The seat takes the name of Attila Kotanyi, a professor whose architectural ideas had a decisive influence in its conception.

Wangen studied the way in which folding seats from the past functioned in order to define the crucial point of the invention: the static nature of the structure which gives total solidity and the free movement of the seat and back-rest in space.

Thus it is not surprising that it was the static principle involved which was protected by patents years before the final design was defined. A system of reciprocally cancelling forces is the differential characteristic by which the Attila is assured of a constant equilibrium no matter which

The unfolded chair seen from various angles.
Dimensions: 73cm height, 63cm width and 56cm depth.
The "Attila" is produced in ash or cherry wood and impregnated with oil in a natural shade or dyed black.

of the multiple possibilities of seating is chosen.

Once unfolded, the seat and backrest of the Attila chair are mobile, and can be adapted to the different positions required by the user. This is due to the fact that the vertice which joins the two planes is not anchored to any support. The chair is made of cherry or ash wood, impregnated with oil. The fittings are of matt stainless steel. Due to the ease of storage, the chair is ideal for use on special occasions.

The experience acquired during the development of the Attila chair was subsequently put to good use in designing a *chaisse longue*, and Wangen also plans to produce a table, an upholstered seat which converts into a table, and a sofa bed. •

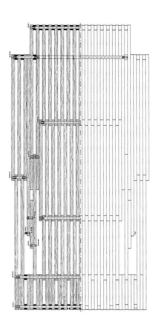

The chair folded.
Dimensions: height
125cm, width 63cm,
thickness 2.5cm.

A reclining version of the
"Attila" chair. The
backrest folds down to
give a horizontal
platform.

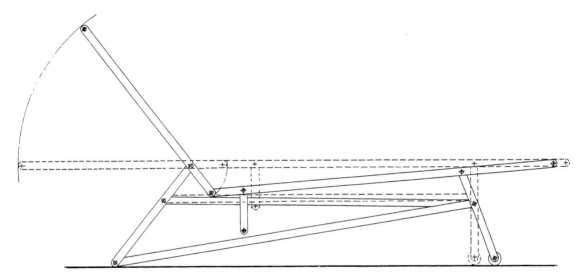

BARBA CORSINI

- A graduate in architecture from the Escuela Superior de Architecture of Barcelona.
- Among his most notable projects: apartments in the attic floor of La Pedrera (Arch. A. Gaudi) in Barcelona, the Victoria Cinema, housing in Badalona, a holiday village in Menorca, a building in La Molina ski station in Spain, and a savings bank in Granada.
- He has designed various pieces of furniture, some of which are in the Design Museum of Barcelona. The "Pedrera" chair forms part of the collection of the Vitra Design Museum.

RODOLFO DORDONI

SIGFRIED BENSINGER

- Germany, 1943.
- After an apprenticeship as a carpenter, studied interior design in the "Werkkunstschule" art school in Darmstadt.
- In 1977, began collaborating with the magazine "Shöner wohnen" as interior designer, and at the same time developed his work as an industrial designer.
- Currently works independently in both furniture and interior design.

MARCUS BOSTCH

- Germany, 1961.
- Studied Mechanics, Arabic and History of Art as well as Industrial Design at the University of Essen. Graduated in 1985.
- In 1991, he created his own studio in Cologne, where he has developed systems of ladders, kitchens, medical products and furniture for various firms including Adams Ladenbau, Cramer and Moormann.
- Since 1995 he has been design adviser for various firms in Manila and Cebu in the Philipines, and has taught in the FH Design School in Cologne.
- His designs have been displayed in galleries and museums in Cologne, Düsseldorf and Frankfurt.

PIERANGELO CARAMIA

- Cisternino,1957.
- Graduate in Architecture from the University of Florence (1984). Master in Urban Design from the Domus Academy (1986).
- Lecturer in L'école Regionales des Beaux Arts of Rennes since 1990 and of the Department of Furniture Design of the Architecture School of Paris-Conflans.
- He has worked as industrial designer in Italy, France, Japan, etc. (Alessi, Cassina, Doublet, Iguzzini, Xo, etc).
- His interior designs include the Bond Street Café, New York; the Le Pigalle café and shop for Alessi in Paris; the rehabilitation of a hotel in Amsterdam and another in Paris. He is currently is designing an office building in St. Petersburg.

ACHILLE CASTIGLIOONI

- Milan, 1918.
- Graduated in Architecture from the Polytechnic University of Milan, 1944.
- Professor at the University of Turin (1970-80) and Milan (1980-)
- Member of the educational committees of design schools in Pasadena (U.S.A.) and Montreaux (Switzerland) since 1985. Honourary member of the Royal Society of Art, London, since 1986.
- Since 1944 he has worked as an architect and designer with many companies including Alessi, De Padova, Driade, Flos, Knoll and Kartell and has received many awards including the Compasso D'Oro in the years 1955/60/64/67/79/84/89.
-His work is on display in museums in New York, London, Zurich, Monaco, Prague, Jerusalem, Cologne and Hamburg.

PEPE CORTÉS

- Barcelona, 1946.
- Studied at the Eina School in Barcelona, where later he would be a teacher.
- His interior design projects include: the "Azulete" restaurant in Barcelona, together with Ò. Tusquets; the "Francisco Valiente" shops in Valencia, with

Eduard Samsó; the "Gambrinus" bar in Barcelona
with Alfred Arribas; offices for "Daniel Hechter"
with Fernando Salas, and the "Tragaluz" restaurant.
- He has produced furniture for B.D. Ediciones de
Diseño, Akaba, Artespaña, GrupoT, Amat and
Technal.
- His work has been awarded prizes on many
occasions by the FAD of interior design.

RODOLFO DORDONI

- Milan, 1954.
- Graduated in Architecture from the Polytechnic
University of Milan in 1979.
- Combines his work as an architect with interior
design, in which field he has collaborated with firms
such as Arteluce, Artemide, Cappellini, Driade, Flos,
Foscarini and Moroso, among others.
- He has created designs for stands, pavilions and
shops for various companies.

SANDRA FIGUEROLA Y MARISA GALLÉN

- Sandra Figuerola, Valencia 1957.
- Marisa Gallén, Castellon 1958.

- Have formed a partnership since graduating in
Fine Arts in Valencia in 1982.
- Members of "La nave" from its formation in 1984
to its dissolution in 1991, thereafter creating the "
"Estudio Ni" with José Juan Belda and Luis González.
- They have worked in industrial, graphic and
fashion design, collaborating with companies such as
Alessi, La Mediterránea and Gandia Blasco.

MICHAEL GRAVES

- Studied Architecture in the University of
Cincinnati (Bachelor, 1958), Harvard (Master,
1959), and in the American Academy in Rome
(1960-62).
- Established his own independent architectural
practise in Princeton, New Jersey in 1964.
- His architectural projects include hotels,
convention centres, institutional buildings, shopping
centres, sports centres, theatres, libraries etc, for
which he has received many prizes.
- His industrial designs have been produced by
Alessi, Steuben, Arkitektura, Swid Powell, Baldinger
and Atelier International.

KONSTANTIN GCRIC

- Munich,1965.
- Apprenticeship as carpenter in the J. Makepeace
School (England, 1984-5) and studied in the Royal
College of Art of London during 1988-90.
- During 1990, he worked in the London studio of
Jasper Morrison.
- In 1991, he established an office in Munich where
he has developed projects in interior and industrial
design for companies such as Arteluce, Cappellini,
Moormann and SCP, as well as various exhibitions.

OLE JENSEN

- Denmark, 1958.
- Studied in the Kolding Art School, Denmark and
the Royal Academy of Arts of Copenhagen (1985-
88).
- Has worked for Royal Copenhagen since 1985.
- Lecturer in the Copenhagen Design School since
1992.
- Numerous exhibitions in Copenhagen, Paris,
Madrid and Barcelona.

AXEL KUFUS

- Essen, 1958.
- Studied carpentry in schools in Kempen and Bad
Wildungen until 1983.
- Has worked with the sculptors R.Mühlemeier
(1979-82) and U. Holthöfer (1984-86)
- Studied Industrial Design in the HDK in Berlin in
1985.
- Since 1990 he has designed products for Atoll,
Cappellini and Moormann in addition to interior
design work.
- Has taught in the Neue Fakultät Gestaltung of the
HAB of Weimar since 1993.
- Has had exhibitions in Kassel, Munich, Hamburg,
Düsseldorf, Stuttgart, Cologne, Berlin and Paris.

VICO MAGISTRETTI

- Milan.
- Graduated in Architecture in the Polytechnic
University of Milan in 1945.
- Member of the Academy of San Luca of Rome
since 1967.
- Has received numerous awards including the Gold
Medal in the IX Triennale of Milan (1951), the Gran

Prix of the X Triennale of Milan (1954), the Compasso d'Oro (1967 & 1979), and the Gold Medal of the Society of Industrial Artists and Designers (London,1986).
- Honourary Member of the Royal College of Art of London and the Royal Incorporation of Architects of Scotland.
- His works have been shown in some of the most famous design shows of Europe, the U.S.A. and Japan, and are on display in various museums such as the Metropolitan and the MOMA in New York.
- He has taught in the Domus Academy of Milan, and is Honourary Visiting Professor of the Royal College of Art of London.
- His professional activity has included architecture, urbanism and industrial design.

PETER MALY

- Trutnov, Czech Republic, 1936.
- After an apprenticeship as a carpenter, studied interior design, graduating in 1960.
- Until he set up his own office in 1970, worked for the magazine "Schöner Wohnen" as designer and editor.
- As well as his design work, he has worked on advertising campaigns and has created stands for exhibitions.
- His designs have been produced by various companies including Cor, Tecta, Interlübke, Reim Interline, Ligne Roset and Knoll, and he has received numerous awards.

ALGELO MANGIAROTTI

- Milan, 1921.
- Graduate in Architecture from the Polytechnic University of Milan,1948.
- Visiting lecturer in various Univerities: Illinois Institute of Technology, Chicago (1953-54); University of Hawaii (1970); Ecole Politecnique de Lausanne (1975); South Australian Institute of Technology, Adelaide (1976); Polytechnic University of Milan (1990).
- He has a long and distinguished career in both architecture and design, and has received many

JAVIER MARISCAL

-Valencia, 1950
- In 1971 he moved to Barcelona to study graphic design in the Elisava School.
- His most famous works include the "Bar Cel Ona" poster (Barcelona, 1979), the "Cobi" mascot for the Barcelona 92 Olympic Games, the corporate logo for Radio Onda Cero (Spain,1990), the "Acuarinto" children's playground for the Huis Ten Bosch theme park (Japan, 1992), designs for the "Socialdemokraterna" political party (Sweden,1993), magazine covers for Apo (Japan), Aldus and the New Yorker (U.S.A.), El Pais Semenal and Casa Vogue (Spain), L'Officiel (France), Time Out and Blueprint (England), and advertising spots for 3M (Japan,1996) and the mascot for the Hanover Universal Exhibition 2000 (1996).

NANI MARQUINA

- Barcelona 1952.
- Studied in the Escuela Masana of Barcelona.
- Dedicated full-time to textile design from 1982 onwards, working for various firms.
- In 1986 created his own company and label, to produce and distribute his own designs.

URSULA MUNCH PETERSEN

- Denmark, 1937.
- Studied ceramics in the Copenhagen Art School (1956-1960), the Escuela de Diseño y Artesenias, Mexico (1968), and the Fine Arts Academy of Copenhagen (1970-72).
- Lecturer in the School of Applied Arts, Copenhagen, since 1973.
- Worked for various companies in the ceramics field before setting up as an independent in 1978.
- Has worked with the firm Royal Copenhagen since 1987.
- Her work has been awarded many prizes in Denmark.